FOUNDATIONS
OF
RELIGIOUS EDUCATION

FOUNDATIONS
OF
RELIGIOUS EDUCATION

Edited by
PADRAIC O'HARE

Paulist Press
New York, N.Y./Ramsey, N.J.

Library of Congress
Catalog Card Number: 78-51591

ISBN: 0-8091-2108-5

Published by Paulist Press
Editorial Office: 1865 Broadway, New York, N.Y. 10023
Business Office: 545 Island Road, Ramsey, N.J. 07446

Printed and bound in the
United States of America

Contents

Preface

RICHARD P. McBRIEN

The maturity of a scientific discipline is measured, in large part, by its readiness to identify and explore foundational questions. In theology the foundational questions are such as these: Is God real? Is the real God available? How is the real God available? How, and according to what rules, can we speak of the real, available God? What is the relationship between our own personal thinking and speaking about God, on the one hand, and the thinking and speaking about God that has gone on for centuries in the broader community of faith, on the other hand?

In religious education the foundational questions are such as these: What is education? When is education "religious"? What is religion? When is religion "Christian" and/or "Catholic"? When is religious education "Christian" and/or "Catholic"? What is catechesis and how is it related to religious education?

So relatively new is the field of religious education that its theorists and practitioners do not always agree on the naming of their common enterprise. Is it simply "religious education"? Is it "Christian education"? "Catholic education"? "Catechesis"? "Religious instruction"? "Christian instruction"? "Catholic instruction"?

The reader will find in this volume advocacies of most, if not all, of the preceding possibilities. And in this dispute over language, there is revealed a deeper dispute over meaning, scope, purpose, and distinctiveness.

As a systematic theologian, I count it a positive development that there has been such a renewal of interest in fundamental theology among many of my colleagues. We are indebted to Karl Rahner, Bernard Lonergan, Edward Schillebeeckx, and others

1

INTRODUCTION

PADRAIC O'HARE

Most persons working in the field of Catholic religious education today know that different views exist about its nature, scope, purposes, appropriate structures, and methodologies. Such diversity could be healthy and creative if these various views, with their assumptions and implications, were clearly understood and could be critically compared. As yet, however, little has been done along these lines and as a result this diversity is as much a cause of confusion as of creativity to both religious educators and those whom they are trying to serve. Ecumenical conversations about religious education are certainly a necessity today. Yet the need is at least equally urgent for critical analysis of the differences existing among Catholics.

To call attention to this **need** and begin to meet it, the Religious Education Institute of Boston College sponsored an "Intra-Catholic Dialogue" on the Foundations of Religious Education, held on the weekend of April 22-23, 1977. Supported in part by a generous grant from the Raskob Foundation, this symposium was designed to give five proponents of differing approaches to religious education an opportunity to present, clarify, and compare their positions in open conversation with one another and with a participating audience.

The five panelists were: Thomas H. Groome, Assistant Professor of Religious Education at Boston College; James Michael Lee, Professor of Education at Notre Dame University; Berard Marthaler, Professor and Chairman of the Department of Religion and Religious Education at Catholic University of America; Gabriel Moran, Director of *The Alternative* and Adjunct Professor of Religious Education at New York Theological Seminary and Boston College; and Françoise Darcy-Bérubé, Assistant Professor in the Institute for Pastoral Ministry at the University of Montreal. The first four panelists had prepared papers in advance, expressing divergent understandings of the nature, purpose, and preferred language for speaking about religious education. Dr. Darcy-Bérubé served as the critical reactor on the panel, and has contributed an essay to the present volume. The proceedings were expertly chaired by Dr. Mary Cove, Director of Religious Education in the Catholic Diocese of Springfield, Massachusetts.

In the pages that follow, a number of highly challenging and disparate ideas and emphases in religious education will be articulated and examined. Thomas Groome will argue the need to make freedom the major paradigm for Christian education and to develop participatory techniques inspired by critical epistomology. James Lee will argue the centrality of technological efficiency in religious as well as all educational enterprises. Berard Marthaler will explore—and ultimately advocate—a socialization model for Christian education. And Gabriel Moran will insist we find a perspective on educational activity in the Church at once concerned for what is particular to our religious community and for the larger world of meaning in which Catholic Christians live.

These and many other theoretical and practical points are made and contradicted. Of immense help to the reader is the final, critical-synthetic essay by Françoise Darcy-Bérubé. While acknowledging many of the finest points in each of the other authors' essays, Darcy-Bérubé will argue that Groome is insufficiently praxeological, Lee insufficiently critical of value-laden social-scientific approaches to the technology of instruction, Marthaler insufficiently attentive to the distinction between religious socialization and Christian faith, and Moran insufficiently specific about the applicability of his thought to age levels of persons.

As the subsequent pages will indicate, the symposium was "heavy going." It was intended to be, and publicized as such, so the frustration felt by some participants during and after the weekend was not a matter of false expectations. It arose rather from the difficulty, common to all but aggravated for Americans, of perceiving the helping relationship between scholarship and the practical order. The simple proposition that conceptual clarity can help make practical action more effective and more faithful to its own intentions seems indisputable. Yet the gap between "theoreticians" and "practitioners" grows not only in religious education but in many endeavors. It is a dangerous development, as much the fault of dogmatic scholars as of anti-intellectual practitioners. The initiation of sustained conversation between the two will be the next great step in the progress of religious education. The first Boston College Religious Education Symposium neither addressed practical questions directly, nor overcame the profound plurality of the academic and ministerial field called "religious education." What it has taken is a step in the direction of doing what the "ministry of scholarship" must always seek to do. The symposium papers have, we believe, appreciably sharpened conceptual clarity about what is at stake in choosing one over another fundamental option for understanding the task of religious education.

Christian Education for Freedom: A "Shared-Praxis" Approach

THOMAS H. GROOME

PART I

IN QUEST OF A LANGUAGE AND PURPOSE

The whole world spoke the same language, using the same words. They said to one another, "Come, let us build ourselves a city and a tower with its top in the sky, and so make a name for ourselves; otherwise we shall be scattered all over the earth." Then the Lord said: "If now, while they are one people, all speaking the same language, they have started to do this, nothing will stop them from doing whatever they presume to do. Let us go down there and confuse their language, so that one will not understand what another says." Thus the Lord scattered them from there all over the earth, and they stopped building the city. That is why it was called Babel, because there the Lord confused the speech of all the world. (Genesis 11:1-9, abridged, New American Bible)

Language

Introduction

The Tower of Babel story makes it sound as if Yahweh was threatened by the unity of his people's language. In that unity they had such power that nothing could stop them "from doing whatever they presumed to do." This people, whose first parents had sinned in wanting to be "like unto God," again needed to be humbled. Perhaps the danger was that if their language remained united then in time they could come to speak the fullness of the Word and thus save themselves. But that was to be the divine prerogative, so Yahweh confused their language.

In the next chapter of Genesis, however, Yahweh makes the promise to Abram that this scattered people will become "a great nation," God's own people. It is to be assumed that as we strive to become God's people, a reality that will not be fully realized until the coming of the Kingdom, one of our tasks is to undo the effects of Babel. The unity of the Kingdom must surely include a unity of language, and the building of that Kingdom will be empowered by clarity and some consensus about the words we use to name our world.

In the common area of concern with which we here occupy ourselves, we are far from consensus on the language we use to describe our task. There is little agreement among us on what we mean by religious education, education in religion, religious instruction, Christian education, catechesis, Church education, etc. Hopefully this symposium may push us a little further away from Babel. At least it may clarify our options. In the interest of doing that I will begin by explaining what I consider to be the three most usable and promising terms as I understand and use them: namely, *religious education, Christian education*, and *catechesis*. Before doing that I want to preface my remarks with two caveats.

First we must avoid an idealist assumption that all our problems will be solved and our task completed if we can only find "the right words." To paraphrase Marx, naming the world is still only preliminary to changing it. While we struggle for greater clarity and consensus we must still get on with our task and not allow the controversy to paralyze us into inactivity.

A second caveat is that each of us must resist the temptation of insisting that everyone else use his/her language under penalty of excommunication from the community of discourse. That would be an oppressive stance and a blatant attempt to "own" our enterprise. In my life I have been greatly enriched by dialogue with people who used a very different language from mine. It is to be hoped that the same can happen here.

Education
Since the beginning of human consciousness, many of the great thinkers and philosophers have articulated a definition or description of education. Perhaps the most influential attempts at

understanding what it is have come from Plato, Aristotle, Augustine, Alcuin, Aquinas, Erasmus, Luther, Calvin, Comenius, Rousseau, Pestalozzi, Herbart, Marx, and Dewey. I have been informed by those people, more perhaps by the Platonic tradition than any other, and have come to the following description. By education I mean the deliberate and intentional attending in the present to the future possibility of the total person and of the community.[1] Education is a concerted attempt by people called educators to enable others with themselves to confront the limit situations[2] of life and push beyond them. Those limit situations may vary from an inability to communicate at the beginning of life to an inability to face finality at the end of it. Since education is intended to push us beyond our present selves and situations, it can be said that, ultimately, all education is a reach for the transcendent.

Religious Education

What do we mean when we preface "education" with the adjective "religious"? The adjective, as it is used in our context here, is derived from the noun "religion." That noun needs to be defined or, at least, the general reality to which it refers needs to be described. David Tracy makes the point, "There is no universal agreed upon simple definition for the human phenomenon called 'religion.' "[3] Robert Bellah, the leading spokesperson on "civil religion" in recent years, defines religion as "a set of symbolic forms and acts that relate man to the ultimate conditions of his existence."[4] There Bellah is being influenced by the thinking of Clifford Geertz.[5] Tracy, grounding it in the concept of the limit situation of human existence, offers the following description: "Employed in our common discourse 'religion' usually means a perspective which expresses a dominating interest in certain universal and elemental features of human existence as those features bear on the human desire for liberation and authentic existence. Such features can be analyzed as both expressive of certain 'limits' to our ordinary experience and disclosive of certain fundamental structures of our existence beyond that ordinary experience."[6] As limits to ordinary experience, Tracy lists finitude, contingency, and radical transience. As fundamental structures of our existence beyond ordinary experience he lists fundamental trust in the worthwhileness of existence, and basic belief in order and value. Between Tracy's and Bellah's definitions there is at least what Tracy would call a "family-resemblance."[7]

Informed by both of them, I understand religion as the constant quest of a person or people to confront and reach beyond the limits of human existence to the ultimate conditions of that existence. But pushing my definition a step beyond either Tracy's or Bellah's statement, I settle for saying that religion is the human quest for the transcendent. The drive within us that impels us on such a quest is the religious dimension of us. (More specific—see notes.)

In the light of this understanding of religion, placing the adjective "religious" before the noun "education" qualifies but does not substantially alter the definition of education already given above. Education and religious education share a fundamental commonality in that both enterprises attempt to empower people to confront the limits of their lives and to reach beyond those limits. That is why Whitehead could write "The essence of education is that it be religious."[8] The same sentiment was echoed earlier by Comenius and in our own time by Moran. "Eventually all education is religious education and . . . religious is not a component or qualifier so much as a test of whether it is education at all."[9] I disagree with Moran, however, in his claim that religious is not a "qualifier" of education. It is a qualifier, not in that it substantially alters the educational enterprise, but in that within the general task of education to confront and push beyond the limit situations of human existence, religious education is a more deliberate attending to the ultimate dimensions of life, that is, the transcendent.

But while the adjective "religious" qualifies without substantially altering the noun "education," the term "religious education" still lacks sufficient exactness to describe the specificity of the task that I see us people here to be about. Indeed, we are concerned with education, and with religious education. But is there not a specificity to what we do that further qualifies our activity beyond both education and religious education?

Looking at my own present historical situation, I find myself, for example, posing the question of how and when to prepare people for the Christian sacraments of initiation. That is an educational and a religious educational question but there is a specificity to it and to the task it poses that neither term adequately describes.

Gadamer, among others, makes the point that the language we use cannot be capriciously chosen. While there is a subjective element to our language, it must also attempt to be an accurate description of the reality outside of ourselves that we are seeking to describe. The term "religious education," because of its lack of specificity, only partly describes what I do. Therefore a more descriptive term is needed. The term I choose is "Christian education."

Christian Education

While we may talk about religion in general as a historical phenomenon, in reality it finds its expression in specific historical manifestations. As Richard McBrien remarks, "there is literally no such thing as religion as such. There are specific religions which participate, to one degree or another, in the general definition of religion."[10] Or as Santayana put it, "Any attempt to speak without speaking any particular language is not more hopeless than the attempt to have a religion that shall be no religion in particular."[11]

In our human history, various traditions of religion have emerged. Each of them, in its own way, is an organized expression of the human reach for the transcendent, an attempt to confront the "throwness" of life and to celebrate a hope in the possibility that our limit situations can be surpassed. If a person draws upon a particular religious tradition to confront the limit situations of life and to pose future possibilities beyond them, then, it seems to me, that tradition should be named. Without such naming the terms used will not describe the reality intended.

In my education, I bring, and invite others to bring, the Christian faith tradition, its symbols, its sacraments, and its rituals to confront the human limit situation of our lives. It is by them that I make some meaning out of my life and have hope in a possibility that transcends my present limits. Thus it seems obvious to name my activity "Christian education."

Another way to state this argument is to return to the definition of education above. To attend in the present to the future possibility of a person and a community is to presuppose a past tradition that is embodied in that present and upon which the future can be grounded. "To lead out" *(educere)* to a future presupposes something from which the leading out is done. My commitment is to the enabling of people with myself to mature in our potential for entering into communion with God and each other through Christ Jesus. It is thus that we can come to live with the glorious freedom of the children of God made possible by that Christ's dying and rising. In this the specificity of my educating derives from the Christian faith tradition. That is the point of departure from which I attempt to lead out. Therefore, it is more accurate to describe my task as Christian education, and perhaps more accurate still to call it "education in the Christian faith tradition," though for aesthetic reasons I prefer the former term.

Such a position is obviously not to equate Christian education with religious education. Unfortunately in much of the literature the terms are often used interchangeably as if the two were synonymous. Rather I am placing Christian education under the umbrella of religious education as a specific expression of the many possible expressions of the human reach for the transcendent.

I am aware of the pejorative connotations the term Christian education can have, especially in some Protestant traditions. For some people it carries unfortunate overtones of indoctrination. Moran, in *Religious Body*, rejects Christian education in Protestantism because it is the activity by which "officials of a church indoctrinate children to obey an official church."[12] (He says that the same activity in Roman Catholicism is called "catechesis.") But I, for one, am not willing to relinquish the term on that ground. Christian education does not have to, and it should not, mean indoctrination. I believe the term can be reclaimed to mean enabling people to live humanly and freely by interpreting and living their lives through the paschal event of Christ in history.

I agree that there are some words that just cannot be reclaimed. They would seem to be inherently oppressive and we must be rid of them. But if we are to jettison all the words in our language that have had a pejorative connotation at one time or another, then we will find ourselves with a greatly depleted vocabulary. For example, the term "black" has often been used to mean something evil or sinister (a blackened heart, a black mark against you) while "white" was synonymous with virtue and purity. The racist connotations of such language are obvious. But rather than expelling them from our language, it is our own false consciousness that must be expelled and our usage of these words that must change. We must come to see that "black is beautiful."

A related objection arises from my proposing the notion of Christian education for freedom (see my title above). If Christian education is synonymous with indoctrination then it surely cannot promote human freedom. Beyond that, both orthodox Marxists and Freudians, among others, would claim that the very use of Christian language militates against the promotion of liberation and human freedom since Christianity is inherently oppressive. I believe that this critique is a dated 19th-century one. It overlooks the early Roman Catholic response to such critique, reflected especially in the great social encyclicals since *Rerum Novarum,* and the Protestant response seen, for example, in the work of Reinhold Niebuhr. It especially overlooks the whole development of critical theology over the past twenty years (for example the work of Moltmann, Metz, Pannenberg, Schillebeeckx, Baum, Gutierrez, etc.) in which the possibility for Christianity to be a critique rather than a legitimation of an oppressive status quo has been rediscovered.

Catechesis

The word "catechesis" comes from the Greek *katechein* which means "to echo" or "to hand down." It is used in the New Testament as an oral instruction in which a very simple explanation (one step beyond the kerygma) was given to the people, as milk rather than solid food is given to children (see Heb. 5:12-14, 1 Cor. 3:1-3). The message was to be "spoken accurately" (Acts 18:25). This oral "reechoing" understanding of catechesis continued in the early Church where it was understood as a verbal exhortation to live a moral life. "Catechesis as oral teaching in the primitive church signified usually a moral instruction."[13]

Attempts have been made to expand the word "catechesis" to mean more than reechoing or handing down. Berard Marthaler states, "I understand 'catechesis' as a process whereby individuals are initiated and socialized into the church community."[14] But that is a definition of "intentional socialization." I do not believe it is possible to redefine the term this far away from either its etymological, scriptural, or early Church roots. I prefer to use it with its original meaning. Thus catechesis becomes, or rather remains, the activity of reechoing or retelling what was handed down to us. In my own methodology it corresponds to Step Three outlined below—the telling of the Christian Community Story. This situates catechesis as a specific activity within the broader concern of Christian education.

Although "religious instruction" is the term favored by one of our symposium panelists, James Michael Lee, I have not dealt with it in the hierarchy of terms outlined above. I do not mean to ignore it. But I find the three terms already outlined sufficient to describe both the breadth and the specificity of our task. For me, at least, the term "religious instruction" is not helpful. I do not prefer it as a sufficiently descriptive term because of its adjective "religious." Like "religious education," it lacks sufficient specificity. I also have reservations about its noun "instruction," at least as Lee uses it. "Instruction" leads inevitably to a teacher/student/schooling mode of education that is too limited for our task as I understand it. Further, if what we are about as Christian educators is seen only as instruction, then there is the added danger, which Lee falls prey to, of talking about manipulating the learning variables to produce predetermined behavioral outcome. Such an approach places the educator in a position of "power over" students' lives. It assumes that this is as it should be, and that such power will always be used justly. It is, however, just as likely to be used for manipulation as for education.

To outline what I mean by these primary designating terms is certainly not to complete the search for a language to empower us in our task. It is my hope that the language I am proposing for Christian education will become evident from its use in the following pages. At the end I will draw more specific attention to the language I have used.

Purpose: For Freedom

I propose that the purpose of our Christian education is to enable others and ourselves to live freely and humanly with the glorious freedom of the daughters and sons of God (Rom. 8:21). Underlying this statement of purpose there are two assumptions about Christianity. (1) Christianity is primarily a way of life—a life-style—a way of being and doing in the world. (2) The Christ who died and rose is the source of hope by which we can come to live as free people.

The first assumption scarcely needs defense. The constant tradition of Christianity from the beginning to the present has maintained that it is not enough to proclaim "Lord, Lord" (Mt. 7:21). The will of God must also be lived in our daily lives. The second assumption is what is more open to challenge. I intend to meet that challenge at greater length elsewhere, but here, due to the exigencies of space, I must be brief.

The general corpus of critical theology already referred to, and especially the various theologies of the liberation motif, have brought to our consciousness the realization that the whole Christ event was one of liberation for us. Let me immediately make it clear that by "theology of the liberation motif" I do not intend the popular identification of that as Latin American theology (see footnote 28 for my criticism of their exclusively economic critique). The general body of critical theology, among which even the work of the later Rahner can be placed, has had a liberation interest. This interest is especially evident in the hope and political theologies, in the feminist and black theologies, and in the Third and Fourth World theologies now emerging.

It may be objected that to refer to Christ as "Liberator" is to manipulate both the Christ of faith and the Jesus of history to suit the needs of our time. This is not the case. It is rather the bringing of a present critical consciousness to reinterpret the meaning of Christ and his dying and rising for us. Undoubtedly this poses a different "hermeneutical framework for interpreting the Biblical and theological tradition afresh."[15] But it is the task of the Christian people in all ages to constantly and critically reclaim their faith tradition in the light of contemporary consciousness. Thus, for example, we read the Gospels for almost two thousand years without ever noticing that Christ's way of relating to women was a radical departure from the culture of his time and a blatant contravening of the sexist mores of his society. It was only when the Gospels were read with a critical feminist consciousness that this was noticed.

If we bring a liberation consciousness to reinterpret two of the traditional titles for Christ, namely Savior and Redeemer, we can exemplify the fact that the work of Christ is one of human freedom. In the history of Western Christianity there have been two principal and equally acceptable models for understanding the meaning of redemption. One (usually called the classical or ransom model) is that Christ died and rose to save us from the powers of evil (Savior). The other (usually referred to as the Latin or satisfaction model) is that he died and rose to pay the price for our sins (Redeemer). Whichever model was used, traditional theology insisted that Christ freed us from our sins and saved us from their consequences.

The problem was, however, that sin was understood too narrowly as a private matter, and salvation too exclusively as an "other worldly" affair. Thus we ended up with the impoverished notion that Christ died and rose to save our individual souls for heaven.

But when we deprivatize sin (and we must to be faithful to the Biblical notion of it), then it is not only a private individualistic affair but also a social reality. Our sins take social form and become embodied in the social structures of our world. "Sin is evident in oppressive structures, in the exploitation of man by man, in the domination and slavery of peoples, races, and social classes."[16] Any social structure that prevents people from authentic union with each other and communion with God is sinful. Thus, when we say that sexism, racism, totalitarian socialism, and uncontrolled capitalism are sinful, we do not only mean that these things are sinful when they occur in the lives of private individuals, but also that the very structures and customs that maintain such activities are sinful.

To deny this is to refuse to see the communal as well as the individual dimension of sin and how they each maintain the other. For example, while it is individual greed that leads to uncontrolled economic exploitation of others, yet that economic exploitation becomes a societal structure (uncontrolled capitalism) that in turn shapes its members in the direction of greed. The two go hand in hand. The dying and rising of Christ are intended to free us from both of them or else his dying was in vain. As Schillebeeckx puts it, "Individually and collectively, man needs emancipation and redemption."[17] And Gregory Baum says, "The salvation of Jesus Christ has a bi-polar, personal-and-social meaning, and any attempt to leave out one pole distorts the original message."[18]

This deprivatizing of sin leads to a desacralizing of salvation. By this I mean that the effects of the redemptive work of Christ are not just for later in heaven—"extrahistorical." While it cannot be completed here, salvation is to begin here. Otherwise it is no more than "pie in the sky." Gutierrez says, "Salvation is not something otherworldly, in regard to which the present life is merely a test. Salvation—the communion of man with God and the communion of men among themselves—is something which embraces all reality, transforms it and leads it to its fullness in Christ."[19]

Seen in this light, the redemptive work of Christ the Savior and Redeemer must be understood as the empowerment of the human struggle for freedom and liberation, a struggle that is to begin in our present even though its completion will be elsewhere and at another time. As Hodgson puts it, "His resurrection is the energizing force in the dialectics of emancipation and redemption by which liberation occurs historically."[20] Thus, as the great Scripture scholar Ernst Kasemann so convincingly argues, "Jesus Means Freedom."[21]

Three Dimensions of Freedom

While freedom is a unity (since we are unities), for the sake of clarity we can conceptually outline three dimensions of it.

First dimension. We will not be entirely free until we come to full union with God. Only there can the human hunger for freedom be fully satisfied. As we struggle toward that end, the highest form of freedom is what I call spiritual freedom—the possibility of entering into communion with God and union with each other.

Thus, the first dimension of freedom is a spiritual one.

Second dimension. But essential to this spiritual freedom is an inner psychological healing of the individual. Without a personal psychological freedom that overcomes the person's alienation from one's self, spiritual freedom is impossible. "Modern man . . . seeks an interior liberation in an individual and intimate dimension . . . on a psychological plain . . . in relation to the real world of the human psyche as understood since Freud."[22] Therefore, the second dimension of freedom is a personal psychological one.

Third dimension. But as indicated by the argument above concerning sin and salvation, there must be a third dimension to this freedom—a social dimension. Hodgson remarks that there cannot be "an inner freedom in the context of an outer bondage and an alien world."[23] Thus, this freedom to which we are called and empowered by Christ's dying and rising means a freedom from sin as it is embodied in the economic, political, and cultural structures of our world. As Rahner puts it, "It is quite impossible in principle for salvation not to be concerned with the social realities within which it has to be realized and made manifest in history."[24]

For the human person freedom is a paradox in that it is not an option. It is an imperative. In Sartre's words, we are "condemned to freedom." To appear to act freely and refuse it is in fact to choose bondage and thus to act unfreely. And since Jesus means freedom, the imperative on those who would be Christian educators is doubly binding.

It is my contention that whenever, wherever, and however people attempt to educate in the Christian faith tradition, the purpose of our educating is to empower the quest for human freedom on all three of the above levels. This is not an easy task. It poses to Christians the challenge of introducing people into their faith tradition but, rather than allowing that tradition to control and determine people's lives, it must be made present as an empowerment toward liberation and freedom. Therefore our content/method must be capable of serving that purpose. I propose an approach of "shared praxis" as one possibility.

PART II

AN APPROACH OF SHARED PRAXIS

Introduction

The term "praxis" would seem to be one of the currently "in" words. It is used frequently today in both theological and educational literature. It is often used, however, by people who obviously intend something very different from its accurate meaning. It is imperative for Christian educators who use it to understand it correctly because it represents a radical epistemological shift and thus should also represent a shift in our way of educating.

Aristotle, borrowing the terms from Pythagoras, said that there are basically three ways of knowing: *theoria*, *praxis*, and *poiesis*. *Theoria* is a contemplative form of knowing, a standing back from to reflect upon the world. The reflection is from a distance and is concerned with knowledge for knowledge's sake. *Poiesis* is a form of knowing but it is more accurately described as an active skill. It is largely unreflective and yet a "knowing" is involved. For example, I know how to swim but I don't think of the principle of gravity, cum water displacement, cum motion, as I swim. If *theoria* is predominantly reflection, *poiesis* is predominantly action.

Oversimplifying in a sense, it is still accurate to say that *praxis* is a combination of *theoria* and *poiesis*. It is not a matter of "looking on," nor is it a question of mindless activity. It combines the twin moments of reflection and participation. *Praxis* is action that is reflectively done, or we could say that it is reflection in action. In this epistemology it is only in being reflectively done that knowledge is known and "knowledge is not knowledge until it is done." Aristotle equated *praxis* knowledge with the living of an ethical life. All three epistemologies are valid ways of knowing, but different, and this is important.

Praxis as a way of knowing has been greatly overshadowed by *theoria* in Western philosophy from Aristotle to the recent past. Theory was seen as something to be known in itself first and then to be applied to practice. This set up a gap between theory and practice that has been a difficult one to bridge. It was Marx, in a dialectical relationship with Hegel's concept of *Geist*, who reunited theory and practice and reintroduced *praxis* as the primary way of knowing. Instead of taking theory as something to be formulated and then applied to practice, Marx reestablished the dialectical relationship between *theoria* and *praxis* and claimed that knowledge is primarily something that is done and is not knowledge until it is done. For Marx, theory emerges from what is being reflectively done and in turn leads to further action, which in turn is reflected upon and so on, in an ongoing dialectic.

There was a problem, however, in Marx's concept of the reflective moment in praxis. The problem was amplified in his followers. Marx was no crude materialist. However, because he saw that which mediates between the subject knowing and the object known exclusively as human labor, and saw the dialectical process as the objectification and reappropriation of that labor, Marx reduced the reflective moment to the level of "production feedback."[26] Habermas points out that for Marx the synthesis that is knowledge "no longer appears as an activity of thought but as one of material production."[27] This bequeathed two problems to later Marxists and to people who would attempt a praxis epistemology. First, it gave too limited a concept of praxis as if all life could be talked of as economic praxis.[28] Secondly, since production feedback was seen to be inevitable, it led later Marxists to reify the evolutionary process and to see it as happening regardless of human cooperation.

The traditional Marxist understanding of praxis has been corrected and broadened by the Critical Theorists of the Frankfurt School and especially by Jürgen Habermas. It is not possible in this short paper to trace the developments. My own understandings of both reflection and action given below are heavily influenced by Habermas and the other Critical Theorists and hopefully the developments will be evident from them. In summary, Habermas expands the action dimension of praxis beyond the technical labor-oriented activity of the person to include the hermeneutical and critical activities of men/women as well. He also reestablishes the necessity of the personal reflective dimension of praxis. He argues for the necessity of critical self-reflective subjectivity that uncovers the interests that lie at the genesis of present action. And, of special importance to our interests here, Habermas also argues convincingly that if the reflection is authentically critical then it is capable of causing emancipation.

I have outlined elsewhere[29] five reasons why a praxis epistemology is more fitting for the task of Christian education than the *theoria* approach that has underlain most of our efforts since Aquinas.[30] (I am also tempted to think that we have had a little *poiesis* epistemology operating in our more recent past with too many unreflective projects, field trips, and collage making.) But a key reason rests on the emancipatory possibilities of praxis to which Habermas points. If the epistemology used in Christian education is an authentically critical one, then it can facilitate the emancipation and freedom I argued for above as the primary purpose of our educating in the name of Christ.

Shared Christian Praxis

Christian education by shared praxis is a group process of critical reflection in the light of the Christian Story and Vision on present action (which embodies one's own story and vision) that is shared in dialogue. I will briefly describe each component of the method.

Critical Reflection. Critical reflection is an evaluative analysis[31] of something, in and of itself, that attempts to unmask by reason the assumptions, interests, and ideologies of our social conditioning. It is an effort to come to awareness of something in its immediacy instead of as it is socially mediated. To use Freire's term, it is a process of "decoding"[32] the reality that society mediates to us in a coded fashion. To effect such decoding it is necessary to return to the genesis, both personal and social, of one's consciousness regarding the issue being reflected upon. This returning to the genesis is a process of remembering. However, the remembering is not a facile "calling to mind" or "noticing." Instead it is a critical remembering (what Habermas calls an "analytical remembering"[33]) that struggles to prevent a reification of our past so that our present and future may not be controlled by that past.

The looking back is done for the purpose of looking forward with imagination rather than with determinism. In this lies the envisioning dimension of reflection by which future consequences of present action are foreseen and chosen—thus, critical consciousness of the present by unmasking its past and envisioning its future. Because of this the process can be emancipatory in that it enables future action to be chosen more freely rather than being determined by the personal and societal pasts that mediate us. It enables us to become creators of our reality and not merely creatures produced by it.

Present Action. The present action reflected upon is that which we are doing physically, emotionally, intellectually, or spiritually. When I speak of present action, however, I do not imply that the reflection is on an historical action that pertains only to the present isolated moment. On the contrary, it is the present as the embodiment of the past and the possibility of the future that the person reflects upon.

The *primary* object of reflection is the subject doing the reflecting.[34] However, remembering that the self is socially mediated, the reflection is *ultimately* on the social context that has done the mediating. Thus the action critically reflected upon must include the social variables (laws, norms, mores, traditions, symbols, ideologies, etc.) that have formed us and find their embodiment in our present action.

Shared. By shared here I mean a sharing in dialogue by the participants of an articulation of their critical reflection on present action. Dialogue is always necessary in any process of humanization because we come to be human by interchange with other people. What I intend by "shared" here is a subject-to-subject encounter of communicating and hearing, best portrayed, perhaps, by Buber's I/Thou relationship.

In the context of Christian education, the content, to call it that, will be the sharing by the participants of their critical reflection on their present actions. But that is not all. I said above that Christian education by shared praxis is a group process of critical reflection in the light of the Christian Story and Vision on present action (which embodies our own stories and visions) that is shared in dialogue. This now brings us to the last two essential components of this approach, namely, the Story and the Vision.

The Story and the Vision: The Sources of Critique

In the Christian faith tradition there is an overall Story that explains where we have come from and an all encompassing Vision that calls us forward. Thus, in a Christian educational context, while the participants reflect upon the story and visions embodied in their present action, those stories and visions must be critiqued in the light of the broader Story and Vision that is Christianity. In the shared praxis of Christian education we look at the genesis of our present action to see if it is faithful to the Story and we look at the vision embodied in our action to see if it is consistent with the Vision. (I return below to emphasize that the Story and Vision must themselves be critiqued by the present. Otherwise they too become controlling ideologies.)

Story. By Story here I mean the whole Christian faith tradition. That Story is the memory of how God has been active in the history of our people and how our people have responded. The Story can be found in Scripture and Tradition (the traditional "fontes veritatis") but it is also congealed in the symbols, the artifacts, the rituals and structures that have developed over our history as a people. Thus, by Story I mean the whole past of our people however that is expressed or embodied. This is why I capitalize the word to distinguish it from story as simple narrative.

God has been active in the past of our people (as in the past of all peoples) and continues to intervene in our present. But the memory of that past Story must constantly be made present if we are to have any basic tools with which to do our interpreting. Otherwise every generation will be reduced, as it were, to "reinventing the wheel," or to trying to get along without it. It is uniquely the task of our educators to make present the Story.

Vision. By Vision I am referring to the Vision of the Kingdom of God in the Hebrew and Christian traditions. The image of it that emerges from the Bible is one of completeness and wholeness. It is the coming of the reign of justice and peace, and the final triumph of love over hate, hope over despair, and life over death. The Hebrew and Christian traditions insist that the Kingdom will be a gift. But while this is true, it does not rob us of our historicity. Our stance toward the Kingdom cannot be one of patient waiting. Instead, we are called to participate in its building.

Drawing on a neo-Marxist understanding of history, we are entrusted with a responsibility for our future. Thus, while the Kingdom can come only by divine gift, the gift comes to us as a grace that enables us to be co-creators of that Kingdom. Rahner points out that while the Kingdom will be a "radical transformation" of history that cannot be caused by human efforts alone, it will not be an obliteration of our human contribution.[35] As the Fathers at Vatican II pointed out in the *Decree on the Church in the Modern World*, the call of the Christian people is "to make ready the material" of the Kingdom (paragraph 38). They added that the "fruits" of our efforts will endure in the Kingdom realized (paragraph 39).

It is clear then that while the Kingdom can come only by the grace of God, we cannot be excused from our human participation in its coming to be. Richard McBrien points out that this is the vocation of the Christian people. "For the Church is perennially the community which must give itself without measure to the building of the Kingdom of God."[36] Because we are called upon to participate in its "building," our present retains its historical significance and must be constantly measured against the values of that Kingdom. Schillebeeckx says, "The new world in Jesus Christ, irrevocably promised and actually on its way, is . . . not a prefabricated reality but is coming into being as an historical process of acting-in-faith in this world."[37] The Christian is called to a faith response that is an "acting-in-faith" on behalf of that "new world." This is why an envisionment of the Kingdom must constantly be made present in the context of Christian education. As we seek to know the Lord (which in a praxis epistemology means to do his will), we must constantly measure and critique our present and the consequences of that present in the light of the overall Vision to which we are called. Again to quote McBrien, "All reality is subordinated to and measured against, the promised future, the fully realized Kingdom."[38] Thus, the Vision with its values of completeness, wholeness, and justice becomes a radical critique of our present political, economic, and social realities insofar as they fail to promote the realization of those virtues.

In Christian education the critical reflection on present action that is shared in dialogue must be based on the Christian Story and Vision. However, it is not enough to stop there either. To do so would be to posit the Story and Vision as fetishized ideologies that themselves control our present. The Story is an ongoing one that needs to be constantly reclaimed and expanded upon by the events of our present. It is still far from completion. Further, the version of it that we have heard has often been distorted. And the Vision is an open one that is constantly being created. Thus, the present, while it is critiqued by the Story and Vision, must also be posed as a critique of the past Story as we know it and as a critique of our present notion of the Vision to whose building we are to contribute. This dialectical relationship between the present and past and between the present and future points to the underlying hermeneutical principle of shared Christian praxis. I call it "present dialectical hermeneutics."

Present Dialectical Hermeneutics

Hermeneutics. Hermeneutics is "the science of interpretation."[39] Etymologically the word comes from the Greek *hermeneuein* which means both "to make clear" and "to interpret." It therefore implies an active search for disclosure and a willingness to share what one has found. Thus, when a group comes together to use a method of shared praxis to do Christian education, they are involved, among other things, in a hermeneutical activity. However, the beginning with the present to look back and to look forward qualifies the kind of hermeneutics that takes place.

Present. I use the word "present" here in what would be taken in popular usage to be a special sense, but I claim it is a meaning that is more faithful to the reality the word represents. By present I mean, not the moment that is distinct from past and future, but rather the point within which the past and future reside. Our typical linear understanding of time does not do justice to this concept of present. The before and after points of chronological time make the present a nonpoint between the two. I prefer to understand the present as the only point that actually exists; there exists within it the consequences of the past and the possibilities of the future.

This notion of present is in the Husserl/Schutz understanding of temporality but it may have been articulated even more clearly by Saint Augustine. In Book Eleven of *The Confessions*, Augustine outlines his position: "If future and past times exist . . . they are there neither as future nor as past, but as present. For if they are in that place as future things, they are not yet there, but if they are in that place as past things, they are no longer there. Therefore, wherever they are, and whatever they are, they do not exist except as present things."[40]

Due to our imperfect language (something Augustine frequently lamented and especially in the context of Christian education[41]), we may need to use words like past, present, and future, but we should do so, says Augustine, only if we intend to mean "the present of things past, the present of things present, and the present of things future."[42]

To summarize, by present I mean the point within which the past is carried forward and the future is anticipated. To reflect on the present is to be like the Roman god Janus—standing in the midst but looking both ways. As a result, the hermeneutics that attempts to interpret our present requires a two-way process that looks from the present to both the past and the future.

In a Christian educational context this means that as we attempt to interpret and come to do the will of God in our present, the past Story of our people must be consciously remembered and the future Vision must be posed as the measure (what Gadamer in his hermeneutics calls "the horizon") of our interpreting. As mentioned already, however, it is not enough to simply impose the Story of the past and the Vision of the future on the present as the unquestioned sources and criteria of its meaning. To embrace the past Story uncritically would be to accept history as completed. But that would be to foreclose the Vision (or at least our part in its building) and would reduce our future to no more than a repetition of our past. In light of this there is need for a dialectic in our present hermeneutics.

Dialectical. The meaning I intend for "dialectical" here is the basic Hegelian one of affirming, denying, and moving beyond.[43] A dialectical relationship must be maintained between the present and past Story because the Story must be critically appropriated and is yet to be completed. A similar relationship must be consciously maintained between the present and future Vision because, while the Vision stands as a critique of the present, it is also being co-created by us with God and thus shaped by our present. As I see it there are four parts to a present dialectical hermeneutics. I will outline each of the parts in an attempt to clarify further what I mean here. The first two pertain to the dialectic between the present and past and the second two to the dialectic between the present and future.

In the dialectical hermeneutic between the present and past Story, the past Story is posed as a critique of the present (part 1). In this it will affirm some of our present, it will deny/condemn some of our present, and it will push us toward action that is more faithful to the Story. But then, for the reasons already given, the present must be posed as a critique of the past Story (part 2). In this there will be dimensions of the Story that we will affirm, dimensions that we must condemn (e.g., the Church's record in regard to slavery), and a call to create upon but move beyond that past. Thus it is not merely asking "what does the past Story say to our present?" but also posing the question "what does the present say to the past Story?"

In the dialectic of interpretation that must be maintained between the present and the future, the future Vision of Shalom is posed as a measure of our present (part 3). Thus, we come to discern what is to be affirmed in our present (there is a sense in which the Kingdom is already among us), we perceive what is to be condemned as retarding the coming of the Kingdom, and we are called beyond our present to a way of living that will be more constructive of that Kingdom. And yet, while the Kingdom is a measure of our present, it is also true that the Vision is an open future that is being shaped by our present. Therein lies the dialectic. Thus, part 4 in the process calls for intentional decision making that takes responsibility for the shaping of the Vision.

Five Steps for Doing Christian Education by Shared Praxis

I have attempted to condense into the last few pages what must surely read like a complex rationale, and one that is a long way removed from an intentional educational situation. In point of fact, I began doing Christian education by shared praxis long before I had such a complex articulation of its theory. In this sense my theory has arisen from my praxis and hopefully has returned to inform that praxis.

The theory/method[44] of shared praxis is presently being piloted in a Washington parish, where it is used in third grade, with teenagers, with young adults, and for adult education.[45] I use an adapted version of it in my undergraduate theology courses here at Boston College. The present process I use to operationalize Christian education by shared praxis has five steps to it. The steps will be done in different ways at different age levels and in differing settings but the same critical principle of present dialectical hermeneutics is necessary, I claim, in any context of Christian education. In an intentional educational setting the process must be focused on a particular topic or issue. Then the steps can be described and done as follows.

Step One: Present Action

The purpose of this step is to bring to group awareness the participants' present action in regard to a particular focus of the Christian faith life. This is done by the participants' articulating their present action in response to the initial focusing question, for example, "What does the Church mean to you?" This is the opening of attention to our present action. It is beginning with the present life situation and experience of the participants.

Step Two: Stories and Visions of Participants

The task here is to return to the biographical and social genesis of the participants' present action ("why do you do what you do?") and to become aware of the future consequences of those actions. This is effected by the participants' critical remembering and telling of the stories, both personal and social, that lie at the base of their present action and attempting to articulate what they envision as the consequences of that action.

Step Three: Christian Community Story and Vision

The purpose here is to make present in the group the Christian Community Story and to imagine the Vision of God's Kingdom as it relates to the topic in hand. This is effected by the educator, or another resource person, retelling the Christian Community Story in regard to the focus of the group, and adding an envisionment of the meaning of this Story in the light of the Kingdom of God.

Step Four: Dialectical Hermeneutic between
the Story and the Participants' Stories
The purpose here is to place the Story and stories in a dialectical hermeneutic with each other. In effect it is an asking of "what does the Community Story say to (affirm, deny, push beyond) our stories and what do our stories say to (affirm, deny, call beyond) the Community Story?"

Thus, this step is a critique of the past Story in the light of the present stories and a critique of the participant's present stories in the light of the past Story.

Step Five: Dialectical Hermeneutic between
the Vision and Participants' Visions
The purpose here is to critique the vision embodied in present action in the light of the Vision of Shalom and to decide on future action that will be constructive of that Vision. In specific groups I have found it helpful to pose the question here as "how is my present action creative or non-creative of the Vision and how will I act in the future?" This step, then, is the placing of present experience in a dialectical hermeneutical relationship with the Vision of God's Kingdom. In this it is a critique of the vision embodied in present action and a decision for future action that will be more creative of the Vision.

The Language of Shared Christian Praxis

Here I wish to do no more than draw attention to the language of this Part II and the language I use to talk about shared praxis. I remarked at the end of the opening section that our search for a language is far from over when we have agreed upon a name for our task. Beyond that we must find a language that empowers us in the doing of it. In light of my position above I claim that it must be a language capable of promoting freedom and liberation. Much of the traditional language of Christian education is oppressive and thus will maintain us in an oppressive practice. To begin with, like a lot of the language of the Christian community it is often sexist. But beyond that, to speak, for example, about "teaching dogmas" or "doctrine" to people is to use words that imply something that cannot be questioned and almost inevitably rules out the possibility of critical appropriation.

In my search for a liberating language I have drawn heavily on the notion of pilgrimage.[46] The very ongoingness and openness of the pilgrimage image can give rise in a "disclosure" rather than a "closure" kind of language.[47] Thus, instead of talking about "teaching doctrines" I talk about "making present a story." Instead of "behavioral objectives" I speak about the visions that call us forward. And the language of *critical* reflection is an attempt to see to it that our discernment of God's will for us in our present is critically appropriated rather than unquestioningly imbibed.

Conclusion

It is some four years since I first read *Pedagogy of the Oppressed* by Paulo Freire. It set fire to my soul. In one way or another, I have been trying to develop and use a praxis method in Christian education ever since. Freire purists will say that I have departed too far from his influence. Perhaps they are right. However, I have done so because of what I perceived to be shortcomings in his method, at least for our context.

I think I grew disillusioned with the catechism approach in second grade when I began to memorize it for the second time through. I used the kerygmatic/salvation history approach in my first years of teaching. But for what I would now call a lack of dialectic between present experience and the past Story, I grew disillusioned with it too.

In the late sixties and early seventies I was greatly influenced and informed by Gabriel Moran. I will always respect him for his many fine insights. For us American Catholics, unduly given to European importations, he has been a creative pioneer. But I moved away from him with *The Present Revelation* (1972). It is not possible to give anything like an adequate critique of Moran's position on revelation here, but I will briefly state my case.

I agree with him that revelation should not be used "as a synonym for sacred scriptures"[48] but by the same token to say that these Scriptures are no more than sources of "inspiration and illumination"[49] is to reduce them to the level of any of the great pieces of literature from human history.

In *The Present Revelation* Moran claims that revelation must be used to refer only to "the relational structure of reality" because "there is no revelation given as a thing from the past."[50] I disagree. Using the terminology of MacQuarrie, I agree that we cannot "narrow the knowledge of God to a single self-revealing act on his part (the biblical or Christian revelation."[51] There is what MacQuarrie calls "general revelation" when contemporary experience takes on "a revelatory dimension."[52] But this "general revelation" does not rule out what MacQuarrie calls "primordial revelation" "on which communities of faith get founded."[53] For "while revelation may be a possibility at any time or place, there are nevertheless 'classic' or 'primordial' revelations that give rise to communities of faith."[54] General revelation from experience and primordial revelation are not contradictory but are intimately related, "for on the one hand, we could hardly believe at all in a primordial revelation unless we had ourselves some present first hand experience of the holy, while on the other hand, the present experience of the community is controlled and given its form by the primordial revelation."[55]

For the Christian faith community the primordial revelation is in Jesus Christ. That primordial revelation can come alive for us again by reflection, in the context of our own experience of our Scriptures. (This is not to equate our Scriptures with revelation nor to claim that Jesus was the only primordial revelation of human history.) I read the later Moran as making an important point in emphasizing "present revelation" but as also overstating the case to the denigration of our "primordial revelation."

The proponents of "intentional religious socialization,"[56] among whom I perceive Berard Marthaler to take his stand, have a strong argument. I would want to be the last person to deny the formative influence of the social context in which we come to be. But because authentic faith communities do not exist in any ideal form but always in some flawed condition, to merely socialize people into what we have will not be enough. An active and deliberate critique in the midst of our communities rather than stronger socialization into them is what is needed.[57] If educators do not promote such critique, who will?

I have also appreciated the insights of James Michael Lee over the years. He certainly wants to take "religious instruction" seriously, and is not reluctant to draw upon the behavioral sciences for the task. But I read him as naively opting for the behavioral sciences as if they are "value free" (Weber's term). He overlooks the whole critique of those sciences, a critique that argues convincingly that the social sciences operate on the interest of "technical control,"[58] "in the service of administration."[59] In a Church that has often erred on the side of authoritarianism, an effective system for manipulating learning variables to produce predetermined behavioral outcomes is more likely to be used for control and indoctrination than for freedom and education.

In conclusion, it is my argument that our Christian education must promote human freedom in its social, individual, and spiritual dimensions. This demands some method that can critically reclaim the past, critically reflect on the present, and create toward the future. I propose "shared Christian praxis" as one possibility.

Afterword

The symposium was a confronting, learning, and growing experience for me. It has forced me to attend to lacunae in my own position in a way that I might not have done otherwise. However, I have decided to let my paper stand as written. This is not to imply that it does not need adjustment or that it cannot be improved upon. There is still much work to be done in my attempt to articulate a praxis approach to Christian education. But, for its day, I still see my statement as an adequate one. I will use this afterword to comment on some points in the paper that I am open to adjusting, to point to some gaps that are left unfilled by the paper, and to comment briefly, in light of the symposium discussion, on my then colleagues, Lee, Marthaler, and Moran.

There are at least two points that I believe need adjusting though as yet I am not sure what the adjustments should be, which is another reason why I allow the original manuscript to stand as written.

In my exchange with Gabriel Moran concernir ; my evaluation of his position on revelation I was opened to the possibility that I am not reading him correctly. But I have struggled with his notion of revelation for some years now and I am still not clear about it. At least some of the blame for that must rest with Moran. In the symposium discussion he claimed to be holding a position on revelation much closer to MacQuarrie's than my paper would indicate. While I am convinced that there are similarities in the two positions, I am also convinced that there is sufficient divergence between them to allow what I wrote to stand as written for now. I continue to see Moran as overstating the case for "present revelation" to the denigration of "primordial revelation" and that is my basic critique of him. (Moran was right when he said that MacQuarrie does not favor the term "general revelation," but he [MacQuarrie] does use it. I was using the term "general revelation" to refer to the notion of the general availability of revelation.)

The symposium side debates also put me in touch with the possibility that some of my interpretations of Moran are as much influenced by his students as by his own writings. At this point I am willing to admit that I am at least confused about his understanding of revelation but I am also anxious to continue a dialogue and come to a better understanding of what he is saying.

A second point in my paper that I have since had doubts about is my imputing of a narrowly theoretical epistemology to Aquinas (see page 22). In my reading since the symposium I have become convinced that such an epistemology cannot be attributed entirely to Aquinas. It is more accurate to trace the current prevalence of such an epistemology to the later scholastics and to the neo-scholastics of our own time.

Turning now to two lacunae in my paper I can say that I was aware of them before the symposium but our discussion there highlighted my consciousness of both of them. They are issues that I intend to deal with at far greater length over the coming years.

In my anxiety to see to it that our socialization processes are critiqued rather than simply done more effectively (which is how I interpret the position of the "intentional socialization"advocates) I am sometimes read as if I am opposed to socialization and the need for a "faith community" in which to grow to Christian faith. Nothing could be further from what I intend. We come to be what we are because of our social contacts and I am convinced that to come to a Christian identity normally requires a Christian faith community. In future work I intend to integrate the socialization perspective more obviously into my approach. But I will never settle for saying that socialization alone is enough (see my remarks on Marthaler below).

A second lacunae in my paper and in my own work thus far is on insufficient attention to the psychological underpinnings of shared praxis and the question of readiness. This problem can be highlighted by the simple question, "Can shared praxis be used with children?" Again, this is an area that I am presently researching intensely and attempting to clarify from my own and my students' involvement in the Christian education of young children. Here I must be brief, but I can say the following. Obviously, critical reflection as I describe it above (the unmasking of assumptions, critiquing of ideologies, exposing of interests, etc.) is not possible for children (and many adults are also incapable of it). But what I describe as critical reflection is an expression of the most critical, thorough, and complete form of reflection. I am convinced that there are stages (perhaps six?) in critical reflection and that some form of reflection is possible and necessary at all age levels. James Fowler is convinced that a form of critical reflection is necessary for the transition between all of the six stages of faith development. Piaget's notion of assimilation and accommodation, of figurative thinking that is imitative and operative thinking that is a "system of transformation," also points to the need for a critical activity at every stage of cognitive development. A description of how this critical activity might be done in the praxis of Christian education with children will have to wait for a later and lengthier work (though good educators have been doing it for years). Meanwhile, I am convinced that if Christian education with children is done by an unreflective "banking method" then those children in adulthood are very unlikely to ever do critical reflection as described in my paper.

Conclusion

There is much more that could be said and I hope to be saying some of it in the years ahead. But in conclusion I want to clarify just two further points.

I do not claim to be proposing a "theory" of Christian education because of the unfortunate dichotomy that exists in our Western minds between theory and practice. Nor do I call my enterprise that of proposing a method (practice) for Christian education for the same reason and for fear that my work will ever be taken as simply another technique. In a sense I am proposing a theory/method and I sometimes call it that in order to capture the twin moments (reflection and action) in the activity of praxis. But a better term for what I am proposing is to call it an approach. By this term I capture and also wish to emphasize that Christian education by shared praxis is as much an attitude, a mentality, an outlook, as it is a theory and a method.

Finally, one challenge that was voiced to my work a number of times during the symposium was that it is unduly cognitive and that it pays too little attention to the affective and behavioral. Nothing could be further from the truth. The central characteristic of a praxis way of knowing is that it is not narrowly cognitive in an intellectualist sense, but rather is a knowing in which reflection, action, and passion are inextricably intertwined. To know in a praxis sense is to reflectively engage in the world. This is why I claim that a praxis epistemology is more suited than a *theoria* one for sponsoring people in Christian faith, which I also see as a form of reflective engagement in reality (rather than as intellectual assent to stated doctrines). If this did not come through in my paper, however, then the fault is largely mine. In future writings I intend to leave no doubt about what I mean by "knowing."

Notes

1. In my understanding of education I must recognize the influence of Professor Dwayne Huebner, Columbia Teachers College. See Dwayne Huebner, "Curriculum as Concern for Man's Temporality," in *Curriculum Theorizing*, William Pinar, ed. (Berkeley, Calif.: McCutchen Publishing Co., 1975).

2. I take the concept "limit situation" from David Tracy. For me Tracy's clearest description of this concept is "a situation wherein we find ourselves not the masters of our fate but radically contingent or limited (boundary situations)." *Blessed Rage for Order* (New York: The Seabury Press, 1975), p. 107.

3. Ibid., p. 92.

4. Robert N. Bellah, *Beyond Belief* (New York: Harper and Row, 1970), p. 21.

5. See Clifford Geertz. *The Interpretation of Cultures* (New York: Basic Books, Inc., 1973), p. 90.

6. Tracy, *Blessed Rage for Order*, p. 93.

7. Ibid.

8. Alfred North Whitehead, *The Aims of Education* (New York: Free Press, 1967), p. 14.

9. Gabriel Moran, *Religious Body* (New York: The Seabury Press, 1974), p. 146.

10. Richard P. McBrien, "Toward an American Catechesis," *The Living Light* 13, no. 2 (Summer 1975): 171.

11. George Santayana as quoted in Geertz, *The Interpretation of Cultures*, p. 87.

12. Moran, *Religious Body*, p. 150.

13. F. X. Murphy, "Catechesis: Early Christian," in *New Catholic Encyclopedia*, vol. 3, p. 208.

14. Berard L. Marthaler, "Towards a Revisionist Model in Catechetics," *The Living Light* 13, no. 3 (Fall 1976): 459.

15. Peter C. Hodgson, *New Birth of Freedom* (Philadelphia: Fortress Press, 1976), p. 208.

16. Gustavo Gutierrez, *A Theology of Liberation* (Maryknoll, N.Y.: Orbis Books, 1975), p. 175.

I would like to add, after this first footnote of Gutierrez, that I too regret in his writings, and in the writings of many contemporary theologians, the "domination of abstract masculine pronouns" (Moran, *Religious Body*, p. 87). However, to dismiss him on these grounds is to refuse to hear a very authentic voice of protest from the Third World, a voice that cries to us in the First World for a redress of our exploitation of these peoples. (The annual return to American drug companies for investments in South America can be as high as 900 percent. See Richard J. Barnett and Ronald E. Muller, *Global Reach* [New York: Simon and Schuster, 1974].)

17. Edward Schillebeeckx, *The Understanding of Faith* (New York: The Seabury Press, 1974), p. 94.

18. Gregory Baum, *Religion and Alienation* (New York: Paulist Press, 1975), p. 211.

19. Gutierrez, *A Theology of Liberation*, p. 151.

20. Hodgson, *New Birth of Freedom*, p. XV.

21. Ernst Kasemann, *Jesus Means Freedom* (Philadelphia: Fortress Press, 1969).

22. Gutierrez, *A Theology of Liberation*, p. 30.

23. Hodgson, *New Birth of Freedom*, p. 70.

24. Karl Rahner, *Theological Investigation Vol. XII, Confrontations* (New York: Seabury Press, 1974), p. 238.

25. As of this writing I have had three articles published on the method of "Shared Christian Praxis," any one of which will explain further some aspect of this Part II. See Thomas H. Groome, "Shared Christian Praxis," *Lumen Vitae* 31 (June 1976); "The Crossroads: A Story of Christian Education by Shared Praxis," *Lumen Vitae* 32 (March 1977); and "The Critical Principle in Christian Education and The Task of Prophecy," *Religious Education* 72, no. 3 (May/June 1977). A fourth article, "Christian Education: A Task of Present Dialectical Hermeneutics," is awaiting publication. I am happy to make it available in private circulation.

26. Trent Schroyer, *The Critique of Domination* (New York: George Braziller, 1973), p. 141.

27. Jürgen Habermas, *Knowledge and Human Interests* (Boston: Beacon Press, 1971), p. 31.

28. This problem, I believe, continues to be a weakness in many of the Third World theologians. As a result they speak only of economic oppression and seem oblivious to oppressions based on sex, race, technology (Alves is an exception there), etc.

29. See Groome, "Shared Christian Praxis," pp. 196-198.

30. I would argue that the epistemology of the early Church's Christian education was largely a praxis one (see Augustine's *City of God*), being a search for spiritual wisdom to be lived rather than for rational knowledge to be known intellectually.

31. I intend a Freudian meaning for "evaluative analysis." This analysis is not simply an intuitive looking at the issue in question, which would be contemplative, but rather a critical analysis of it that bares the social influences that are formative of the present action.

32. Paulo Freire, *Pedagogy of the Oppressed* (New York: Herder and Herder, 1970), pp. 77-118.

33. Habermas, *Knowledge and Human Interests*, p. 301.

34. See Jose Ortega y Gassett, *What is Philosophy?* (New York: W.W. Norton, 1960), p. 216.

35. Karl Rahner, "Christianity and the New Earth," *Theology Digest* 15 (Winter 1967): 275-282.

36. Richard P. McBrien, *Do We Need the Church?* (New York: Harper and Row, 1969), p. 134.

37. Schillebeeckx, *The Understanding of Faith*, p. 11.

38. Richard P. McBrien, *The Remaking of the Church* (New York: Harper and Row, 1973), p. 76.

39. Richard E. Palmer, *Hermeneutics* (Evanston, Ill.: Northwestern University Press, 1969), p. 33.

40. *The Confessions of St. Augustine*, John K. Egan, trans. (Garden City, N.Y.: Doubleday and Co., 1960), p. 285.

41. See St. Augustine, *The First Catechetical Instruction*, Joseph P. Christopher, trans., (Westminster, Md.: Newman Bookshop, 1946), p. 15.

42. *The Confessions of St. Augustine*, p. 291.

43. It should be noted that the popular understanding of Hegel's dialectic as thesis, antithesis, synthesis, is not accurate and does not capture what Hegel intended by the dialectic.

44. I often use and write the term "theory/method" thus in an attempt to capture the twin moments of action and reflection involved in praxis.

45. My "Crossroads" article is a detailed description of how I used "shared Christian Praxis" in an adult education setting.

46. The "Crossroads" article also elaborates further on the use of "pilgrimage language."

47. See Ian T. Ramsey, *Models and Mystery* (London: Oxford University Press, 1964).

48. Gabriel Moran, *The Present Revelation* (New York: Seabury Press, 1972), p. 227.

49. Ibid.

50. Ibid., p. 118.

51. John MacQuarrie, *Principles of Christian Theology*, 2nd ed. (New York: Charles Scribner's Sons, 1977), p. 53.

52. Ibid., p. 251.

53. Ibid., p. 90.

54. Ibid., p. 143.

55. Ibid., p. 448.

56. This phrase was first used, I believe, by John Westerhoff. See John H. Westerhoff and Gwen Kennedy Neville, *Generation to Generation* (Philadelphia: United Church Press, 1974), p. 19.

57. See my article "The Critical Principle in Christian Education," *Religious Education* 72, no. 3 (May/June 1977), for a more detailed critique of the "intentional socialization" approach.

58. Jürgen Habermas, *Knowledge and Human Interests* (Boston: Beacon Press, 1971), p. 309.

59. Jürgen Habermas, *Theory and Practice* (Boston: Beacon Press, 1973), p. 208. See also Max Horkheimer, *Critical Theory* (New York: Herder and Herder, 1968), p. 244.

Key Issues in the Development of a Workable Foundation for Religious Instruction

JAMES MICHAEL LEE

Basic Terminology

Crucial to any field of activity, and especially to scientific activity, is a clear, unambiguous understanding of and agreement upon basic terminology. Unanimity on terminology is necessary if a field is to achieve adequate self-definition. It is necessary to attain unambiguous communication among those working in the field. Finally, it is a necessary ingredient in the generation of fruitful theory and practice. Basic terminology lies near the very foundation of fundamental issues in any field of activity and in any scientific undertaking. Consequently, I am commencing this essay with some fundamental definitions, issues, and proposals involved in religious education terminology.

Behavior is the generic term describing any activity in which an organism engages. Human behavior is classified into three discrete functional groups: cognitive, affective, and psychomotor. Life-style behavior can be described as the functional integration or fusion of cognitive, affective, and psychomotor behaviors into a particular pattern of conduct.

Learning is a term that describes any change in behavior. Learning is verified on the criterion of whether or not a change in behavior has been observed.

Education is the broad process whereby a person learns something. Whenever a person's behavior undergoes change he is being educated. Consequently, education can be said to be taking place during most waking (and possibly some sleeping) moments of a person's life. This vast breadth of educational experience accounts for the fact that moments of leisure, of reverie, of fellowship, of hooliganism, of love, and so on, are sometimes more educative in the life of an individual than moments of structured education enacted in formal settings.

Instruction is the intentional process by and through which learning is deliberatively brought about in an individual in one way or another. Instruction in formal settings (much as in schools) is a highly focused system of complex, planned, organized, systematic, purposive, deliberative, and interrelated learning experiences that, in concert, bring about desired behavioral changes in an individual. Instruction in informal settings (such as the home) is generally less focused with regard to the characteristics delineated immediately above.

Religion is that form of life-style which expresses and enfleshes the lived relationship a person enjoys with a transpersonal being as a consequence of the actualized fusion in his self-system of that knowledge, belief, feeling, experience, and practice that in one way or another are connected with that which the individual or society perceives to be divine. This definition is a behaviorally oriented one. It thus represents an attempt to move away from a notional definition and toward an operational one.

Religious education is that broad process by which a person learns something that he or society perceives to be generically related to God. As the grammatical structure of the term suggests, "religious," the adjective, modifies or specifies the noun "education." Language generally is a verbal reflection of reality. This indicates that religious education derives its basic form and operational principles from that which is inherent in and proper to the educational process. Religious education is nonconfessional in nature; it specifies only that mode of education whose outcomes are perceived to be generically related to the divine. Functionally considered, there are three distinct modes of religious education: religious instruction, religious guidance, and the administration of religious education.

Religious instruction is the intentional process by and through which learning outcomes perceived by the individual and society to be generically related to God are deliberatively brought about in an individual in one way or another. Religious instruction is thus synonymous with the teaching of religion. As the grammatical structure of the term suggests, the adjective "religious" serves to modify or specify the noun "instruction." Language customarily is a verbal reflection of reality. This indicates that religious instruction derives its basic form and operational principles from that which is inherent in and proper to the instructional process. Religious instruction is nonconfessional in nature; it specifies only that mode of education whose outcomes are perceived to be generically related to the divine.

Christian education is that mode of religious education whose outcomes are perceived to be behaviors claimed by one or another Christian denomination as being either (1) specifically and distinctly Christian, or (2) congruent or compatible with Christianity. Conservatively oriented Christians appear to hold the first of these; liberally oriented Christians seem to lean toward the second. From the standpoint of logical terminology, it is more accurate to refer to Christian education as Christian religious education.

Christian instruction is to religious instruction what Christian education is to religious education. From the standpoint of a logically developed terminology, it is more accurate to refer to Christian instruction as Christian religious instruction.

Catholic education, logically speaking, should be defined as that specific mode of Christian education whose outcomes are perceived to be behaviors claimed by the Catholic Church as being either (1) specifically and distinctly Catholic or (2) congruent or compatible with Catholic behaviors. However, as typically used by Catholic ecclesiastical officials, Catholic educational officials, and the majority of Catholics, the term "Catholic education" is synonymous with "Catholic schooling." In customary Catholic usage, namely in sectors of the Church not directly engaged in activities that instruct or guide persons in the attainment of specifically religious outcomes, the term "religious education" is usually used to denote (1) formal religion classes and religious guidance given in Catholic schools, and/or (2) formal religion classes and religious guidance conducted in programs outside the confines of the Catholic school. Both the terminological identification of Catholic education with Catholic schooling, and the terminological illogic in viewing Catholic education as basically different from Catholicly-oriented religious education should be eliminated if the field of religious education and its subdivision, Catholic education, are to achieve clarity. I therefore propose what appears to be logical and commonsensical, namely that the term "Catholic education" be used to refer to that form of religious education whose outcomes are perceived to be Catholic. Such a definition has significant administrative implications in addition to its scholarly ones. I further propose that the term "Catholic schooling" be used to indicate the total educational program which is offered in formal educational institutions conducted under church auspices or otherwise organically related to church activity.

Catechesis is a term used exclusively by some Catholics in place of the term "religious instruction." The word "catechesis" is derived from the Greek, meaning "to inform by word of mouth," or "to sound down," and usually refers to oral instruction, especially as given to beginners. In the early Church, catechesis appears to have constituted the second phase of the kerygma-catechesis-didascalia cycle of religious instruction. In the catechetical phase, the Apostles and their followers provided verbal, generally cognitive instruction about the rudiments of the Christian religion (although some doctrinal tenets were introduced also). I firmly believe that when the term "catechesis" is used today, it should be reserved exclusively to refer to the second phase of the kerygma-catechesis-didascalia cycle employed in the religious instruction program of the early Church. And I strongly urge that the terms "catechesis" and "catechetics," when intended to denote contemporary religious education or religious instruction, be completely abandoned. I recommend this for five reasons. *First*, the term "catechesis/catechetics" inherently suggests more of a pedagogical strategy (verbal transmission/proclamation) than a field or a major subdivision of a field. To equate religious education or religious instruction with any one pedagogical strategy—and a unidimensional, limited, and relatively ineffective one at that—is to rob the enterprise of a great deal of its potential success. *Second*, there seems to be no consensus—and possibly little interest in achieving consensus—on the meaning of the term "catechesis/catechetics." Disagreement and confusion about the meaning of basic terminology is fatal to any field. *Third*, "catechesis/catechetics" is an archaic term, one bearing little or no relevance to the modern world. *Fourth*, "catechesis/catechetics" is a separatist term in an age when Protestant and Catholic religionists and educators are increasingly dialoguing together, researching together, and developing instructional strategies and methods together. "Catechesis/catechetics" is a uniquely Catholic term that must continually be translated for Protestants and others involved in or interested in religious education. *Fifth,* the term "catechesis/catechetics" is a useless one and serves no purpose. It obfuscates and fogs up what should be relatively easy, clear, and readily understandable terminology. If religious education is ever to achieve the status of a professional field of study and of work, it must employ a terminology that is at once understandable to all who use it and systemically related to the terminology of the field most closely associated with it. In the field of education, the terms "education," "instruction," "moral education," "moral instruction," "religious education," "religious instruction," "mathematics education," "mathematics instruction," and so forth have definite, specified, and agreed-upon significations. There is no need to resurrect archaic terms like "catechesis/catechetics" to denote meanings for activities for which proper and clear terms already exist. That beings should not be multiplied without necessity is a principle no less applicable to contemporary Catholic religious education than it was for William of Ockham.

A Workable Foundation for Religious Instruction

As its title suggests, this essay focuses on religious instruction. It does not deal expressly with those two other major task-based subdivisions of religious education, namely religious guidance and the administration of religious education.

The only workable foundation for religious instruction is that found in the content of religious instruction. The content suggests what the foundation must be. As I shall discuss later, the content of religious instruction is the religious instruction act. Every fruitful activity, every fruitful formulation, every fruitful conceptualization of religious instruction, either flows toward or flows out of the act. Indeed, it is incorrect to speak of religious instruction content (structural *or* substantive) except as it dynamically exists in the act, or, more accurately speaking, *as* the act.

Any theorizing about religious instruction that does not make the religious instruction act the starting point and the finishing point is but a background, a backdrop; it is not foundational theorizing; it is not theorizing about the foundations of religious instruction.

The foundation of religious instruction can be found only in the religious instruction act precisely because religious instruction is nothing more and nothing less than the religious instruction act itself.

Unfruitful theorizing about religious instruction as well as sterile and blind-alley religious instruction practices result almost totally from their being dislocated from the religious instruction act. The more religious instruction theory and practice are continuously grounded and centered in the religious instruction act, the more fruitful they will be.

Theory and Practice in Religious Instruction

Theory and practice constitute the basic ways of looking at a human activity. The nature and character of a particular activity determine the nature, character, and operational axis of the theory and practice that flow from it.

As emphasized previously, the content of religious instruction is the religious instruction act itself. Religious instruction *is* the religious instruction act. Therefore all religious instruction theory and practice must in some way flow directly out of and flow directly into the religious instruction act. The fruitfulness of theory and proposed practice in the work of religious instruction varies inversely with the square of their distances from the religious instruction act.

It is more precise to characterize theory as fruitful than as right or correct. This is because theory is basically a functional affair. A theory is "good" when it is fruitful with respect to practice.

Theory exists in dynamic interaction with practice. Practice is a real being; theory is a logical being. Practice is what occurs; theory is a grand hypothesis about why and how practice occurs or will occur. A theory is, therefore, always tentative.

Theory has three principal functions, all related to the understanding and enrichment of practice. First, theory tentatively *explains* the underlying reasons why a practice occurred as it did. Second, theory tentatively *predicts* if/when a future practice will occur, and how effective a future practice will be if/when it occurs. Third, theory tentatively *verifies* whether or not a practice has actually occurred and whether it was really successful in terms of its objectives. In short, theory serves to interpret and correct existing practice as well as to generate new practice.

If a theory is to be fruitful, then it must be built on a base appropriate and congenial to it. If a theory of dental practice is to be fruitful it must flow from physiological and engineering bases, and not from linguistic bases. If a theory of number is to be fruitful, it must flow from a mathematical basis and not from a physiological or engineering basis. If a theory of religious instruction is to be fruitful, it must flow from a basis that is inherently connected to the effective functioning of the religious instruction act. Now the fundamental and essential characteristic of the religious instruction act is to deliberatively facilitate learning outcomes perceived to be religious. Religious instruction practice is said to exist to the extent to which it facilitates outcomes perceived to be religious. Put negatively, if practice fails to facilitate an outcome, or if practice facilitates an outcome other than one perceived to be religious, then this practice is not religious instruction practice. This brief analysis suggests that the only appropriate basis for religious instruction is social science, because social science alone has the power to fruitfully explain, predict, and verify the effectiveness or noneffectiveness of religious instruction practice. No other science possesses this capability.

The success of religion teaching varies directly with the degree to which the source of a theory of religious instruction, the theory itself, and the procedures employed in its practice are all in congruence with one another. For example, to be effective, a set of instructional procedures must flow from teaching theory. If a person seeks to derive effective instructional practices from inappropriate theories such as a theory of plant growth, a theory of historical research, or a theory of divine grace, his efforts will not bear fruit. An effective physician treats a patient on the basis of practices derived from medical theory, and not from a theory of grace. So too an effective religion teacher instructs a learner on the basis of practices derived from a teaching theory, and not on a theory of grace. Medical theory is grounded in natural science; teaching theory is grounded in social science. To ground medical theory in social science is to render it unfruitful. To ground teaching theory in natural science—or theological science—is to render it unfruitful.

Foundational Issues—How Foundational?

In terms of foundational issues, how radically different from each other are the viewpoints expressed in the four principal essays in this book? In my opinion, these four viewpoints,[1] far from being foundationally in conflict, are in fact complementary. Each of the four chapters deals with a different level of pedagogical affairs. Berard Marthaler's essay deals with the *goals* of religious education. He proposes the traditional goal of socialization, one that is still eminently valid for much of present-day Catholic (as well as Protestant) religious education. Thomas Groome's essay, while dealing with the goal of freedom, nonetheless is primarily devoted to advancing a pedagogical *method*. The shared-praxis method is simply a variation of the action-reflection teaching method and quite possibly is useful for those religious instruction activities that are almost totally cognitive-based and cognitive-thrusted. Gabriel Moran's essay focuses on the importance of *language* in religious education. Verbal content certainly is an important and powerful content in religious education, a content whose force as a content is frequently overlooked or downplayed by religious educationists and religious educators alike.

Upon careful examination, none of these concerns—goal, method, language—is foundationally foundational. This statement does not in any way deny or minimize the great importance of goal, method, or language. Rather, it indicates that goal, method, and language flow from a foundation rather than constitute a foundation.

What makes a goal pedagogically valid and operable? What

conditions must be present to make a particular method work? What accounts for the differential effects of language when it is used in different circumstances and situations? It is the task of foundational theory to adequately explain and resolve the questions of "What makes . . .?" "What conditions . . .?" "What accounts for . . .?" Foundational theory addresses itself to the foundations of any and all goals, methods, and languages.

It is to the basis, the foundation of religious instruction, that my essay is directed. It attempts to examine and answer the fundamental issues of when, why, which goals/methods/languages to use in a given religious instructional situation. My essay explores the foundational basis for explaining, predicting, and verifying the appropriateness and effectiveness of *any and all* goals, methods, and languages.

At its most basic level, a foundation is that which discloses and explains both what a reality is and how it functions. In terms of religious instruction and indeed of all religious education, to know the foundation is to know the elemental form and workings of the field. To grasp the foundation of religious instruction is to grasp its basic principles. These principles are operative in all goals, methods, and languages that religious instruction might be called upon to assume in any given concrete situation.

The real foundation of religious instruction is far more basic than statements about goals, methods, or languages. The real foundation of religious instruction is a set of statements that show *why and how* these goals, methods, and languages *work*. The real foundation of religious instruction is a set of statements that can *predict* when the goals, methods, and languages will be effective and when they will be ineffective.

Any real foundation of religious instruction (and of religious education) must have at least two distinct and essential properties. First, it must be comprehensive, that is, it must be able to explain, predict, and verify the entire spectrum of religious instruction goals, methods, languages, structures, and so forth. Second, it must be systematic in that it must be able to relate all the goals, methods, languages, structures, and so forth, to each other in a way that all these elements at once work together in an interactively organic unity and reinforce each other in an integral, advancing manner.

In short, Marthaler's socialization goal, Groome's shared-praxis method, and Moran's language emphasis all rest upon some foundation. Each of these flows from a foundational theory, a theory that forms the foundation or basis for the goal, method, and language. I believe that the goal, method, and language emphasis advanced by Marthaler, Groome, and Moran respectively are all based on the foundational social science approach. Berard Marthaler virtually states as much in his fine essay. Socialization is a path of human interaction, observes Marthaler, and it is social science theory that is the appropriate foundational one to explain, predict, and verify the dynamics and outcomes of human interaction. For his part, Groome proposes an instructional method. The method Groome advances, namely shared praxis, is an interactive one and therefore flows out of foundational social science theory. It is social science to which Groome must look to find out when to use his shared-praxis methodology, how to use it, how to ascertain its effectiveness, and why it works or does not work in a given situation. Finally, Moran's language emphasis as he uses it in a religious education context flows from foundational social science theory, since it is social science that at bottom explains the actual power, pitfalls, limitations, and workings of language as a content.

Foundational theory, as I emphasized earlier in this essay, must be comprehensive—it must include any and all goals, methods, languages, structures, contents, and so forth, in whatever area it is foundational. This basic principle holds true just as fully in the religious instruction field as in any science, discipline, or field. Therefore, socialization, which is admittedly the traditional and probably the most widely embraced goal in religious instruction today, cannot be truly foundational because there are circumstances in which other, nonsocialization goals are more appropriate and more important as, for example, the goal of a nondomesticated freedom. This is one of the key points made by Ivan Illich and Paolo Freire. Furthermore, the shared-praxis method, which quite possibly is helpful in achieving cognitive outcomes, cannot be truly foundational because many (and, I suspect, most) circumstances demand the use of affectively based and especially life-style based methodologies. It would be tyranny and shortsightedness to claim that any one method is the only method; method, after all, is not a foundational foundation, but only one praxeological instance derived from this foundation.

Some Observations on the Social Science Approach to Religious Instruction

I advocate the social science approach to religious instruction because this is the only possible foundation for the development of fruitful religious instruction theory and practice. Conversely, I reject the theological approach because it cannot possibly serve as an adequate basis for explaining and generating religious instruction activities. The theological approach forms a background, a backdrop for religious instruction, but it cannot and it does not serve as its foundation. Theology is vitally important in that it constitutes some of the crucial subject matter content. But theology is *in se* impotent to assist the religion teacher in determining the curricular design, scope, sequence, and balance whereby the entire range of content is put into a form that is optimally teachable and learnable. Theology is unable to offer relevant prescriptions to the religion teacher on how to analyze and control his pedagogical behavior, how to arrange learning experiences in that kind of programmatic form that will most successfully bring about the objective(s) sought, how to develop procedures for the supervision of religious instruction, how to effectively evaluate learning outcomes, and the like.

There is no empirical evidence to suggest that religion is learned in a manner substantially different from the way learning occurs in other areas. Nor is there any empirical evidence to suggest that the attainment of learning outcomes perceived to be religious is facilitated in a substantially different manner than is the case with other kinds of outcomes. Learning takes place according to the regular laws and progressions of human activity. This is as true for religious learning as it is for any other kind of learning. It is therefore not only incorrect but actually damaging to the religious instruction enterprise to assert a priori that religion is somehow taught and learned in a manner apart from the laws and progression of human activity. Indeed, such assertions amount to a spookification of a highly important area of instructional endeavor.

The objective of the first phase of my professional career has been to erect an overarching theoretical approach to religious instruction. This approach has certain characteristics that I believe are absolutely necessary if it is to be optimally fruitful. First, this overarching approach continuously flows out of and into the core of religious instruction, namely the religious instruction act. Second, it is built on the only foundation that is capable of generating successful theory and practice, namely that of social science. Third, it is comprehensive; that is, it seeks to deal with all the phenomena falling under the entire spectrum of religious instruction. Fourth, it is systematic in that it arranges phenomena, data, laws, and subtheories into an orderly pattern in which relationships are specified and interrelated.

I set forth my version of the social science approach to religious instruction in a trilogy. The first volume, *The Shape of Religious Instruction*, establishes the basic rationale for the social science approach. The second volume, *The Flow of Religious Instruction*, deals with the structural content of religious instruction. The concluding volume, *The Content of Religious Instruction*, treats of the substantive content of the field. Taken as a unit, the trilogy forms what I believe is the first attempt ever made to construct a comprehensive, systematic, integrated macrotheory of religious instruction. I sincerely hope that similar attempts by other religious instruction specialists will follow in the years and decades ahead.

The fruitfulness, the "goodness," of any approach to or any overarching theory of religious instruction can be gauged by how it holds up when tested by certain key "litmus-paper" criteria, including the following: (1) What kind of theoretical formulation is it? Is it a theological theory, an instructional one, a religious instruction one, or what? (2) Is it internally consistent? (3) Is its methodology appropriate to and adequate for the religious instruction phenomena with which it purports to deal? (4) Is it comprehensive? Does it deal with the entire spectrum of phenomena in the field of religious instruction? (5) Is it systematic? (6) Is it capable of generating fruitful religious instruction practices? (7) Is it capable of predicting the occurrence and relative effectiveness of the phenomena that can be considered as properly belonging to the field of religious instruction? (8) Is it capable of verifying the existence and effectiveness of religious instruction phenomena? I hasten to note that these criteria are the ones classically employed to ascertain the merits of any theoretical approach of theory vis-à-vis the field in which it claims to operate.

An individual wishing to compare the relative fruitfulness and worth of the theological approach to religious instruction with the worth of the social science approach should rigorously apply these criteria to both approaches. I predict that the results of such a comparison will clearly show the theological approach to be inappropriate and unfruitful, whereas the social science approach is appropriate and fruitful for the work of religious instruction.

The Content of Religious Instruction

The content of religious instruction is the religious instruction act, nothing more, nothing less.

By empirically examining the religious instruction act and then reflecting on what I discovered as a result of my investigation, I have been able to identify the two principal components of the religious instruction act, namely structural content and substantive content. In terms only of the religious instruction act itself, neither of these two contents can be said to enjoy independent or autonomous existence. Each of these two becomes a content of religious instruction only at such a time as it is compounded with the other to form the religious instruction act.

The structural content of religious instruction is the teaching process. This content assumes many and varied shapes, depending upon the dynamic interaction in the religious instruction act of the teacher, the learner, and the environment—as each individually and in concert interacts with the substantive content. The structural flow that a religious instruction episode will take depends in large measure on the kind of pedagogical approach, style, strategy, method, technique, and steps the teacher employs—both as these are internally integrated taxonomically and as they interact with the learner, the environment, and the substantive content. Structural content comes into existence as a content of religious instruction only when it is compounded with substantive content to form the religious instruction act. One cannot teach nothing; one can teach only some kind or pattern of substantive content.

The substantive content of religious instruction is religion. This content assumes many and varied shapes, depending upon the emphasis and arrangement of the sub-contents contained in substantive content. On the basis of empirical investigation, I have identified eight discrete subcontents of substantive content: (1) product content; (2) process content; (3) cognitive content; (4) affective content; (5) verbal content; (6) nonverbal content; (7) unconscious content; and (8) life-style content. The first six of these subcontents can be conveniently paired. All eight are present to some degree in every enactment of substantive content during the religious instruction act. Because the structural content of religious instruction is religion, it follows that the substantive content of religious instruction is not theology. Religious instruction is not theological instruction. Religion is a way of life; theology is a science. They have different axes, different methodologies, and different goals. Substantive content comes into existence as a content of religious instruction only when it is compounded with structural content to form the religious instruction act. Religion, of course, has existence after the manner of the arrangement of its subcontents; it exists apart from the religious instruction act. But as the substantive content of religious instruction, it has existence only when it is dynamically and existentially compounded with structural content in the religious instruction act itself. Religion as being taught, then, is not the same substantive content as religion in some other form.

The Purpose of Religious Instruction

The purpose of a being is to adequately actualize what it is. Thus the primary purpose of religious instruction is to successfully facilitate outcomes perceived to be religious.

Religion is a life-style; it is a way of life. Therefore the primary and overarching outcome of religious instruction is that the learner's life-style be modified along desired religious lines. Other vital and essential outcomes such as cognitive and affective ones assume roles and importance in keeping with the degree to which they foster and enhance religious life-style behaviors in the learner's life.

The Relationship of Theology to Religious Instruction

In terms of the structural content of religious instruction, theology plays no direct role. There is no such thing as a teaching technique that is distinctively Christian, much as there is no such thing as a farming technique or a dental technique that is distinctively Christian.

In terms of substantive content, the role of theology is determined by the manner and the extent to which it is related to religion—not simply to religion in general, but more importantly to religion as it is conceptualized and takes shape as the substantive content of a particular religious instruction act. With respect to the substantive content of religious instruction, theology is not thrust toward itself as in the case of theological instruction, but rather is thrust toward religion. Theology is not religion; religion is not theology.

In terms of religious instruction, structural content and substantive content come into existence only as they are dynamically compounded in the religious instruction act. With respect to the act, then, the role that theology assumes is directly in proportion to the degree to which it is relevant and appropriate in fostering the facilitation of desired religious outcomes.

The religious instruction act is not a vehicle or instrumentality for inserting theological content into the learner's mind. Religious instruction is not a handmaid or messenger boy of theology. Theology exists in the religious instruction act as that which is shaped by its ongoing dynamic interaction both (1) with other dimensions of substantive content and (2) with the learner, teacher, and environment, as all these in turn dynamically interact in the religious instruction act.

A norm establishes the bases for an activity and then verifies the extent to which the activity has implemented these bases.

While theology does serve as a kind of norm for religious instruction, it by no means constitutes the exclusive or even primary norm. It is the entire process of religious instruction that, by virtue of its proper and interactive nature, exercises the essential normative function. Religious instruction is not theology; therefore its norms cannot be properly or primarily theological. Whatever normative role theology does play in a particular religious instruction act is determined by the role and the coloration it assumes in that act. If some person or group imposes theological norms on religious instruction, he or it does so not by virtue of norms derived from or proper to the religious instruction process itself but by virtue of norms derived from or proper to some other form of activity. The latter are imposed on religious instruction from the outside. Such outside norms are typically political in origin and orientation—political in the broad sense of the term.

Teaching Theory

Theory exists to enrich practice, to improve it, to make it work. If theory is to perform this vital, highly practical role, its nature and characteristics must perforce be such as to be directly and properly related to the practice it is intended to enhance. If the teaching process falls under the purview of social science, then it is obvious that only a theory derived from social science is adequate to explain and generate effective new pedagogical practices. Theories of teaching that are derived from theology are neither appropriate to nor effective for the teaching of religion.

Any adequate teaching theory must specify the major pedagogical variables operating in the instructional dynamic, and indicate their relationship both with themselves and with the outcomes their interaction is intended to produce. An adequate teaching theory must also have the inherent power to explain, predict, and verify pedagogical process.

The only kind of theory capable of adequately performing the functions mentioned in the preceding paragraph is teaching theory. And teaching theory is and can only be derived from social science. In *The Flow of Religious Instruction* I construct and describe one kind of teaching theory I believe to be especially fruitful.

So-called teaching "theories" derived from theology or from

good will lack the power to explain, predict, and verify pedagogical practice. Such "theories" fail to tell the teacher what specific pedagogical practices to use. They do not help the teacher to generate specific effective new practices. In *The Flow of Religious Instruction* I identify seven of the most prevalent pseudo-theories proposed by theologically oriented religious educationists and educators: the personality theory, the authenticity theory, the witness theory, the blow theory, the dialogue theory, the proclamation theory, and the dedication theory. The blow theory, for example, claims that learning outcomes are not directly facilitated by the teacher but rather by the Holy Spirit who blows where he wills. The dedication theory claims that it is the teacher's dedication that is the primary explanation accounting for learning, while the witness theory posits the religion teacher's Christian witness to be the key variable explaining the entire range of pedagogical practice. It well may be that the religion teacher's personality, his Christian witness, his dedication and the like do constitute significant variables in the religious instruction act. But this assertion is far different from claiming that any one of these variables has the comprehensiveness, the power, or the appropriateness to serve as theory that can explain, predict, and verify all kinds of religious instruction practice.

Teaching theory is not learning theory standing on its head. Teaching theory is praxeological theory; learning theory is event theory. Teaching theory tells how a teacher can make a learning outcome occur. Learning theory explains how a learning outcome actually did occur. Teaching theory is prescriptive; learning theory is descriptive. But teaching theory and learning theory flow from social science; they do not proceed from theological science.

Some Major Tasks of Religious Instruction

One major task of the field of scholarship called religious instruction is to put religion into a form in which it is teachable and learnable. There can be no workable basis for religious instruction that does not systematically and comprehensively take into account and delineate the manner in which religion can be rendered optimally teachable and learnable.

Another major task of the field of scholarship called religious instruction is to scientifically examine and study the teaching-learning process. There can be no workable basis for religious instruction that does not systematically and comprehensively examine the many variables operating in the teaching-learning process, that does not investigate the interaction among these variables, and that does not analyze the structure of the theory that explains, examines, and verifies the teaching-learning process.

Finally, a major task of the field of scholarship called religious instruction is to treat of the significant problems and issues involved in the here-and-now improvement of religion teaching. There can be no workable basis for religious instruction that does not comprehensively and systematically deal with, and indeed generate, programs and procedures that can be empirically demonstrated to be of significant assistance in helping to improve the here-and-now effectiveness of religion teaching.

The three criteria mentioned above are useful ones to keep in mind when assessing the fruitfulness and worth of any existing or proposed basis for religious instruction.

Some Bogeymen

A bogeyman is an invented demon or concocted sinister force that a parent invokes to frighten a child into submission, or that a demagogue or a ruling clique devises to discredit and anathematize persons or views he or it opposes. Unhappily, certain religious educationists of the superficial sort, instead of carefully analyzing and critically testing the validity and fruitfulness of the social science approach to religious instruction, have resorted to inventing bogeymen by which they hope to discredit it. Four such bogeymen are freedom, manipulation, positivism, and behaviorism.

The first bogeyman that certain persons invoke against the social science approach is that of freedom. The social science approach, some of its critics claim, minimizes or abrogates freedom in the religion lesson. But like all bogeymen, this charge is a spurious one; it has never been proved in the slightest. Because the only workable foundation for religious instruction is that found in the religious instruction act, it is in the context and enfleshment of this act that the charge of anti-freedom must be examined. The social science approach empowers the teacher to analyze and then shape his pedagogical activity. In other words, the social science approach enables the teacher to be free because freedom comes only when a person both knows what he is doing and can shape or control what he is doing. Anti-freedom comes about when a person is led by forces of which he is not consciously aware or that he cannot shape. The theological approach cannot really lead to freedom in the religion lesson because its very theological nature is inherently unable to empower the teacher to analyze and shape his pedagogical activity. Another important consideration worth mentioning is that of the construct of freedom versus the actuality of free behaviors. Critics of the social science approach level the abstract construct "anti-freedom" at the social science approach. But a construct is only a logical being; it has no real existence. What is real, what is important, is an actual specific behavior that is free or unfree. It well might be that there is a positive correlation between the advocacy of the abstract construct "freedom" and the strictures placed on an individual's free behaviors by advocates of the abstract construct "freedom." Of all political leaders, it is the dictators who talk most glowingly about the abstract construct "freedom" while allowing the citizenry the least amount of free behaviors. Few state constitutions in the 20th century contain so many glorious statements about freedom as does Stalin's 1936 USSR constitution, and few governments ever permitted so few free behaviors as the Stalin government regulated by this constitution. Concrete behaviors, not abstract constructs, are where true freedom or anti-freedom is to be found.

The second bogeyman is that of manipulation. The social science approach, some claim, results in the learner's being manipulated against his will. Like all bogeymen, this charge is hokum—and low-level hokum at that. Any approach (be it the social science approach or the theological approach), any strategy (be it the transmissionist strategy or the structured-learning-situation strategy), and method (be it the problem-solving method or the so-called shared-praxis method), can be manipulative if the teacher or curriculum builder wishes it to be so. Effectiveness enhances the power of that which is effective to be manipulative—or nonmanipulative. The social science approach, when properly enacted, is eminently effective in religious instruction. In the final analysis, manipulativeness and nonmanipulativeness lie in the hands of the teacher and curriculum builder, not in the approach. What we are considering here is the penultimate or even prepenultimate consideration, namely the tendency or proclivity of the approach in itself to lead to manipulativeness or nonmanipulativeness. The theological approach to religious instruction has the strong and indeed almost inevitable tendency to lead the teacher to be manipulative because in truly following this approach the teacher must blindly appropriate pedagogical procedures drawn from social science in order to teach the lesson. (Theology, quite obviously, cannot generate pedagogical procedures because such procedures fall outside its purview and competence.) Consequently, the theological approach is inherently uncritical in terms of the linkage between theory and practice; manipulation typically is the fruit of this kind of uncriticalness. The social science approach to religious instruction, on the other hand, enables the religion teacher to be nonmanipulative (if he so desires) simply because the approach from which both theory and practice of religion teaching are drawn is one and the same, namely social science. The theological approach does not provide the teacher or curriculum builder with the pedagogical tools necessary to prevent the lesson from becoming manipulative. The social science approach, on the other hand, provides the teacher and curriculum builder with these pedagogical tools. It is up to these practitioners to decide and enact teaching behaviors that are manipulative or nonmanipulative.

The third bogeyman that certain individuals invoke against the social science approach is that of positivism. These critics claim that the social science approach to religious instruction is positivistic. Such an allegation clearly indicates that those who make it are either ignorant of the nature of positivism or are unaware of my own version of the social science approach—or both. Some of the basic tenets of positivism are as follows: Metaphysics does not exist; God either does not exist or he is unknowable; theology is nothing more than superstition; all claims about knowledge of transcendence must be rejected. Positivism is a philosophical system, one that I personally reject. I affirm the validity of metaphysics in areas in which it is competent. I affirm the existence and knowability of God. I affirm the validity of theology—indeed, I contend that theology quite possibly is a science, a claim that accords more scientific worth to theology than even many Christian theologians would admit. I affirm the validity of knowledge of transcendent beings and forces. Like almost all Christians, I do accept certain principles of positivism such as the emphasis on experience. But to accept certain principles is in no way tantamount to accepting the entire philosophy of positivism, much as acceptance of the notion of extroversion-introversion necessitates the acceptance of Carl Jung's system of psychotherapy. The social science approach is value-free, so it can be used by a positivist or by an antipositivist. My own version of the social science approach is clearly nonpositivistic.

The fourth bogeyman is behaviorism. Some critics allege that the social science approach to religious instruction is behavioristic. This charge reflects poorly on the literacy level and intellectual capability of those who make it. Anyone who has read even as much as a few pages from a behaviorist's work and from my own writings would recognize immediately that fundamentally, behaviorism and I are very much opposed. Behaviorism is a philosophy that represents one form of positivism. Behaviorism rejects mind. Behaviorism rejects soul. Behaviorism rejects the unconscious as a postulate. Behaviorism rejects feelings and states of mind. Behaviorism rejects God. Behaviorism rejects theology as a valid and worthwhile enterprise. Behaviorism rejects the positing of any dividing line between man and brute animals. My own version of the social science approach as developed in my books, in my university courses, and in lectures, conferences, and workshops in the United States and abroad repeatedly, clearly, and at length affirms all the above tenets that behaviorism rejects. To be sure, I do emphasize behavior. But to claim that emphasis on behavior makes me a behaviorist is nothing more than sheer stupidity or bias. A moral theologian, a priest in the confessional box or in the reconciliation room, a traffic officer, a cooking teacher—all these people emphasize behavior, but this fact does not make them behaviorists. The religious instruction act is a set or pattern of cognitive, affective, and life-style behaviors. Therefore, to understand and improve the religious instruction act one must concentrate on the specific behaviors that comprise it.

A final note is in order concerning bogeymen and those religionists and educators who concoct them. Most religious educationists were trained as theologians; indeed, most religious educationists are clergymen. These persons have come to believe that in one way or another theology comprises their profession, their self-identity, and the self-identity of the Church and of all humankind. Most religious educators have been taught or otherwise influenced by these religious educationists to believe that "to proclaim the Good News" is to proclaim theology. It is therefore not surprising that persons with this background and interest simply do not and often cannot understand social science in general and the social science approach to religious instruction in particular. Social science operates at a different level from theology; it has different interests and different parameters. But the theological world view conditions the holder of this world view to regard the whole world from a theological perspective. Carl Jung expresses the situation well when he observes in his autobiography that "theological thinkers are so used to dealing with eternal truths that they know no other kinds. When the physicist says that the atom is of such and such a composition, and when he sketches a model of it, he too [like I, Jung] does not intend to express anything like an eternal truth. But theologians do not understand the natural sciences and, particularly, psychological thinking. The material of analytical psychology [a mode of social science], its principal facts, consist of statements—of statements that occur frequently in consistent form at various places and at various times." We all remember the bogeymen some theologians used to erect against psychology, such as the ones invoked against psychological screening of religious candidates, personality tests, intelligence tests—bogeymen like positivism, behaviorism, interfering with God's grace, invading an individual's privacy. These same bogeymen are now being resurrected in certain

circles against the social science approach to religious instruction. Just as the bogeymen created to destroy psychology were all
disposed of, so too, slowly but surely, are the bogeymen concocted to disparage the social science approach being discredited.

Conclusion

Throughout this century, Catholic religious educationists
and educators have only rarely considered the foundational foundation of their endeavors. Two reasons can be offered for this
most unfortunate phenomenon. First of all, a comprehensive and
systematic formulation of the foundational foundation of religious
education is not exciting to most persons. The presentation of
new proposals such as the nonschool model, the advocacy of
tantalizing ideas such as liberation-oriented religious education,
or the rediscovery of the importance of adult religious
education—all these are inherently more likely to catch the fancy
of religious educationists and educators than more seminal and
more scientific foundational theorizing. Important and interesting
though these new proposals might be, they are no substitutes for
foundational theory. For after all, it was the foundational theorizing of Plato, Aristotle, and Aquinas—theorizing at once comprehensive and systematic—that profoundly shaped the world
and provided solid bases for fruitful scientific and human development. There were more exciting and more *au courant* thinkers
in those days than Plato, Aristotle, and Aquinas. But the seminal
and foundational influence of Plato, Aristotle, and Aquinas
endures, while the more exciting and flashy figures of their day
are by and large forgotten. Catholic religious educationists seem
to be unwilling or unable to squarely face foundational theory.
They seem to operate at a more superficial, often more flashy
level, preferring ideas or proposals of a lesser though perhaps a
more immediately glamorous order to the depths of foundational
theory. It is as if Catholic religious educationists were chemists
basing their whole field on speculations concerning new combina-
tions of molecules to form more eye-catching plastic toys instead
of devoting their attention to foundational atomic theory.

In the last two decades many important advances have taken
place throughout the country in the area of Catholic religious

education and religious instruction. Often these advances were made at great sacrifice. Yet the lack of a comprehensive and systematic theoretical base has made it difficult for the field to consolidate its victories. The consequence of this lack of a comprehensive and systematic theoretical base is that these victories have to be won over and over again in every new educational encounter, in every new family setting, in every new classroom situation, in every new chancery situation—and by every individual.

It is my conviction—a conviction clearly supported by virtually all the available research evidence—that the social science approach forms a firm and fruitful foundation out of which religion teaching can effectively operate. From a personal as well as a professional standpoint, my work and my vision have always centered on the prophetic role that religious education and religious instruction must play in the Church. As I see it, the most prophetic thing I can do for the field is to construct a comprehensive and systematic foundational theory for religious instruction, for only in this way can the field at once hasten and harvest the future.

Note

1. At the time Dr. Lee wrote his essay, Dr. Darcy-Bérubé's critical essay was not yet composed.

Socialization as a Model
for
Catechetics

BERARD L. MARTHALER

Recent literature in religious education journals of one kind or another indicates some confusion over terminology. If it were simply a matter of semantics, a glossary could straighten out the matter. The terminological differences reflect diverse views about the nature of religious education, its goals, objectives, and methods. Sometimes—in my view, most often—it is a matter of emphasis and priorities; at other times it is a question of defining the discipline. It is the latter question that most interests me, but I realize that one cannot proceed to that point without first entering into the thicket of definitions and technical terms.

The way one defines the discipline has practical ramifications in every area. It affects one's visions as well as one's strategies for religious education at the local level. It shapes the design of the graduate programs in which the professionals in the field are trained. It defines the relationship of religious education to other disciplines—theology, liturgics, the social sciences, education, and so forth. The need to have a clearer identity was made evident not long ago at a meeting on the catechesis of children and youth sponsored by the department of education of the United States Catholic Conference.[1] The meeting presented an unusual opportunity to carry on interdisciplinary discussions among men and women interested in various dimensions of religious education. While the participants were predominantly Catholic, there were a few Protestants and one Jew. Religious educators and social scientists confronted one another. They were broadly representative of the field: They came from schools and CCD programs; the social sciences; they were publishers, researchers, and administrators. But many participants felt that the full potential of the meeting was never realized for want of some common understanding of the goals, objectives, and methods of religious education. The group did not speak a common language nor operate with commonly shared assumptions. In a sense the meeting simply mirrored the actual conditions of the field.

It is the purpose of this paper (and I suppose of this symposium) to sketch a model that will elucidate the nature of religious education and provide a basis for interdisciplinary discourse. I use "model" as a heuristic device to disclose the way selected phenomena interact and relate to one another. Models of their nature focus on selected sectors of reality, but some models are more comprehensive than others.[2] The adequacy of a model is measured in pragmatic terms, that is, by its usefulness in interpreting data and establishing patterns of meaning. It is my contention that a socialization model is useful for explaining and interpreting many of the varied activities that are carried on in the name of religious education.

Although the word may have a strange ring in church circles, the socialization process has been operative in the Christian community since two or three first gathered together in Jesus' name. Insofar as it was an intentional process, socialization was traditionally called *catechesis*. Nor is religious education as socialization unknown among modern authors. It was the model underlying Horace Bushnell's idea of "Christian nurture." While C. Ellis Nelson does not use the idiom of social science, he in fact describes socializaton into the church community in *Where Faith Begins*. John Westerhoff uses both the term "socialization" and the socialization model to explain the dynamics of religious education in *Generation to Generation* and most recently in his *Will Our Children Have Faith?* It is a model that social scientists like Herve Carrier, Andrew Greeley, and Merton Strommen understand and, more often than not, operate from when they undertake research in the field of religious education.

In the following pages I first explore what is involved in the notion of socialization in general, drawing heavily on the social sciences. Second, I show how various activities, formal and informal, associated with religious education are illuminated in themselves and in their relationship to one another by the socialization model. Third, I briefly sketch some of the implications in this approach to religious education.

I. Socialization

Though philosophers and pedagogues as far back as Plato carried on sophisticated discussions about various phenomena of socialization, the term itself is relatively new. It began to appear with some frequency in the writings of social scientists less than a century ago, and according to Clausen it was not until 1939 that it came to be at all widely used in its present sense.[3] Although the definitions of socialization are as numerous as the authors who write on the subject, there is a common denominator in all the descriptions and theories, namely, the interaction of an individual with a collective. The collective may be the nuclear family, a voluntary society, a cultural tradition, or any kind of community of humans. The individual may be a child or an adult, a normal person or a deviant, a willing agent or unwitting participant. In short, every human being, except perhaps the feral child, is consciously or unconsciously a product of socialization. It must be stressed, however, that socialization is interaction: The individual is not simply a bit of clay to be molded by society, but rather an actor who while acquiring personal and social identity influences the group. A child is not simply a tabula rasa that mysteriously responds to the stimuli of adults. Nor are adults fixed and stable factors in a child's world, but are themselves likely to change under the impact of their offspring's challenge.[4]

The number and variety of definitions of socialization reflect the different concerns and foci within the social sciences themselves. Psychologists and psychoanalysts discuss socialization in terms of personality theory, impulse control, ego identity, and the many other factors that contribute to tension or compatibility between the individual and the social environment in which he or she is situated. The sociologist concentrates more on institutional structures, the societal apparatuses that shape the roles expected of the members of a particular group. The anthropologist focusing on cultural traits of one kind or another studies the means by which traditions, customs, and behavioral patterns are transmitted from one generation to another.

Modern psychology is in reality a galaxy of subfields. It incorporates theories of learning and personality as well as stage theories that seek to explain cognitive and moral development. It deals with ego identity and motivation and other aspects of the human psyche. Psychology studies the influence of every imaginable stimulus on human behavior. Psychology understands socialization in a general sense as the development of the individual as a social being with emphasis on the consciousness of self in relationship to other selves. While many psychologists operate within a socialization model, socialization is not a principal focus of research in child psychology, social psychology, and some personality theories. Even in these subfields, however, researchers and theorists have not shown "major interest in the larger process by which an individual is prepared for full participation in adult life."[5] Thus for all the contributions made by the different branches of developmental psychology with its concentration on conditioning experiments, learning theory, and the measurement of attributes of the child, it has for the most part neglected the crucial influence of social interaction and the transmission of culture. One noted exception is Erik Erikson who while concerned with the development of one's self-concept recognizes the importance of the interplay of psychosocial phenomena.

By way of contrast relatively few sociologists regard small children as proper subjects for study except as members of a family, peer group, or some other social unit. Sociology focuses on group relationships and the ways in which they influence the individual. It is concerned with social control and such agents of socialization as the family, school, church, mass media, and so forth. It sees socialization as the process whereby individuals are assimilated into and brought to conform to the ways of the social group to which they belong.

While psychology and anthropology, emphasizing as they do personality and cultural transmission, concentrate more heavily on the study of childhood socialization, sociologists show greater interest in adult socialization. Sociology studies the processes whereby personnel are recruited and trained to fill positions in the societal structures: how one acquires and is influenced by his or her role of parent; how one assumes a professional identity and finds that his or her attitudes and behavior are shaped by the role of doctor or lawyer; how sex roles are assigned, and so forth. In fact, sociologists in the classic tradition generally understand adult socialization in a restricted sense so that it means little more than the acquisition of social and occupational roles.

Anthropologists, however, understand socialization in a more basic sense. They see it in terms of culture and even use "enculturation" and "acculturization" as synonyms for socialization. (The former describes the initiation of a "cultureless" person into the patterns of meaning and expected behavior of a particular adult society; the latter describes the transition of an adult from one culture to another.) Culture is the key word. It comprehends the explicit and implicit values and patterns of meaning embodied in configurations of behavior, social institutions, and all the traits and artifacts that give a particular group its distinctive identity. They are the symbols that constitute and give expression to a culture. Thus culture is understood as a comprehensive symbol system that gives meaning and value to every aspect of social living. The anthropologist who is interested in the socialization process studies how the culture is transmitted from generation to generation by means of the symbols.

These three approaches are delineated for purposes of study and research. Even though psychologists, sociologists, and anthropologists focus on different aspects of the process and use different methods, they complement one another. In the concrete, socialization is all of a piece. If one takes a phenomenological approach socialization is seen as a dialectic, an interaction between the objective world in which one finds him/herself and the subjective world of the individual with his/her particular angles of vision. Both worlds are very real. They shape one another. Society exists, write Berger and Luckmann, "only as individuals are conscious of it," while on the other hand, "individual consciousness is socially determined."[6] It is in the interplay of the objective and subjective worlds that groups and individuals construct their symbol systems, grow to self-awareness, and take on their particular identities. It is through this "symbolic interaction" that an individual comes to recognize him/herself as a male or female, as an American in the 20th century, perhaps as a Catholic Christian, and in all the secondary roles that one acquires by reason of state of life, occupation, and situation in time and place.

Socialization as Dialectic

Social scientists generally recognize that socialization takes place in a fundamental dialectic. Berger and Luckmann, who use a phenomenological rather than an empirical method, describe the dynamics of the process as three "major moments": (1) externalization, (2) objectification, and (3) internalization.[7]

Externalization is an anthropological necessity. A human being cannot but pour him/herself out into the world in which he/she is situated. While the relationship of the human being to a specific environment is a given, it is not permanently fixed. Humans struggle to shape the world in their own image and to fit it to their own needs. Building on the physical universe, societies construct a human world we call culture. Although culture becomes "second nature" to humans, it can still be distinguished from them in the sense that it is the product of their own activity and ingenuity. The preservation and transmission of culture depend upon the ability of peoples to maintain specific social structures and ideals. Seen in this light the world as it is known by human beings is not a static, fixed entity, but the product of the interaction between the physical universe, the culture, and the drive on the part of human beings to externalize their inner needs and desires.

Objectification is a corollary of externalization. When we speak of externalized products of mental and physical activity, we imply that they have attained a distinctive existence apart from their producers. They are like works of art, the painting that exists after the painter dies, the music that continues to be played in a different way from what the composer intended. Thus the socially constructed reality takes on a facticity of its own, it is something "out there." It consists of objects, patterns of behavior, social structures, meanings, and so forth, that are capable of resisting the desires and designs of their creators. "Although all culture originates and is rooted in the subjective consciousness of human beings," note Berger and Luckmann, "once formed it cannot be reabsorbed into consciousness at will."[8]

A special case of objectification is the human production of signs, the carriers of meaning. All objectifications are susceptible to use as signs even though they were not produced with this intention (e.g., a weapon made for hunting animals may become in certain circumstances a sign for violence and aggressiveness). Language, however, is a system of verbal and/or nonverbal signs for the avowed purpose of self-expression—of transmitting thoughts, information, and meaning. Language possesses an inherent quality of reciprocity that distinguishes it from all other sign systems. As a network of words, grammatical constructions, and gestures it is external to the individuals who use it while at the same time it has a formative effect on their thinking and manner of expression. Language forces one into patterns of meaning, but it also opens the possibility of transcending the concrete and particular. Language objectifies the shared experiences of a community, making them available to all the members present and future. Sophisticated practitioners of the language arts can construct extensive edifices of symbolic representations that interpret the objectifications of everyday life and form them into configurations that bring out their significance. It is an axiom of modern sociological tradition "that human action is never simply behavior, but behavior plus meaning. Meaning is constitutive of the human world in which we live."[9] Historically, religion, philosophy, and art have provided the most important symbol systems in the social construction of reality.

Internalization is the term used to describe the reassimilation into consciousness of the objectified world of meanings. It occurs in such a way that the structures of the external world come to determine the subjective structures of consciousness itself. Although individuals are born with a proclivity, even a need, to be socialized, it is only to the extent that they internalize the values and attitudes of the milieu in which they find themselves that they are considered full-fledged members of society. In the sense that socialization connotes a sharing of common meanings and values it is the basis that permits the members of a particular group to understand and communicate with one another.

Identity Formation

Cultural patterns and social institutions function as formative agents of an individual's self-image and world view. Or to put it another way, identity is a phenomenon that emerges from the dialectic between the individual and society. In the course of appropriating the language, institutionalized values, and objectified meanings of a culture or society one acquires a sense of belonging. As one becomes older and gains some degree of autonomy, one becomes more or less free to filter the values and attitudes of the group, but much continues to be dictated by the accident of birth. (A college education, for example, does not have the same importance for the ghetto child that it does for the son or daughter of a university professor.) Society assigns a name and sometimes a fixed role in life. These designations define the individual's place in the world. As one accepts (or rejects) the identification and the roles assigned by the culture and society, one acquires a social identity. To the extent that a person internalizes and consciously appropriates this social identity, it becomes inseparable from his/her self-image.

Every society instinctively, if not deliberately, seeks to form its young and its proselytes according to a predetermined archetype of what a loyal member should be. It inducts new members not by a mechanical process that would stamp an image on them as in minting coins or religious medals. Even a totalitarian society wants to win minds and hearts. The convergence of one's social identity and personal self-image emerges more from a dialogical process in which the socializee is an active participant. The conversation usually begins at home and continues in school with the "significant others" in one's life. An individual's social identity reflects the attitudes taken by the mother, the father, the teacher, and later by one's peer group. In time an individual may come to have a different self-image from the one adults tried to impose on him/her as a child but these initial experiences leave a lasting imprint.

Society carries on this dialogue at various levels and in a

number of ways. Two of the principal ones have already been discussed. One way is to assign a social identity to an individual with the expectation that he/she will internalize it. A person becomes what he/she is named. A child consistently described as an Orthodox Jew learns to regard him/herself as an Orthodox Jew and comes to know in a preconceptual way what is expected of one who would be an Orthodox Jew. A second way in which a group socializes its members is by encouraging the socializees to appropriate as their own the symbol system that embodies the meanings it shares and gives expression to its values and attitudes. The Orthodox Jew learns of the temple, the Torah, and the Talmud, of the Sabbath, Yom Kippur and Passover, of kosher food, of the Holocaust, and of the many other practices and sacramentals that constitute Jewish tradition. The self-image of a Jew is inseparable from these symbols. They define his/her social identity and give meaning and purpose to his/her world. A Jew writing an autobiography cannot tell his/her story without at least some reference to the history of the Jewish people.

Socialization, at least in the case of the young, begins before the socializees are capable of normal reasoning, and in every case involves more than purely cognitive learning. Even the adult learner and, *a fortiori*, the child, identifies with the significant other in a variety of emotional ways. Berger and Luckmann go so far as to say "there is good reason to believe that without such emotional attachment to the significant others the learning process would be difficult if not impossible."[10] Furthermore, the symbols that are the carriers of traditions and meanings have rich connotations that speak to the whole person, not just the mind. They evoke what no concept can, namely, the polyvalent meanings that a person attributes to a particular act or event. Religious symbols in particular seek to disclose the ultimate meaning of human existence. They are not simply incidental to one's social identity but are so interwoven with one's self-image that an individual who has internalized them has no personal identity without them.

Gregory Baum sums up the function of religious symbols in the socialization process as follows:

Ever since we are little children, we are exposed to values, norms, meanings and purposes, through our parents and the social institutions (including language) of which they are part, so that we assimilate a system of symbols long before we achieve the rational maturity to be critical and search for our own values. Even when we reach this stage of maturity, we are never empty subjects in search of new meaning, for woven into our personal, intellectual, and emotional structure are the meaning and values in which we participated as we grew up. We are able to re-educate ourselves, but our deep conviction or doubts about love, trust, fidelity, and the orientation to grow are so deeply tied into our personal being that it is only on these and through these that we modify our conscious purposes. Man's relationship to the deepest dimension of his life remains inevitably implicit; it can never be conceptualized; it can only be spoken of in symbols.

The symbol, then, expresses man's relationship to the ultimate in his life. The symbol makes this relationship more conscious and communicable and thus intensifies man's involvement in it.[11]

Before moving from this discussion of socialization in general to a consideration of the specialized form of religious socialization we call catechesis, it might be well to add that the socialization process is never completed. The dynamics of externalization, objectification, and internalization continue through one's lifetime. Erik Erikson's well-known "eight ages of man," each with its successive crisis, illustrates that a person continues to grope for identity. In every stage of life one restructures past identity images in the light of an anticipated future.

II. Catechesis[12]

The socialization model brackets out aetiological, theological, and epistemological considerations. It takes the present realities of everyday life as its starting point. In dealing with the Christian religion it begins with the phenomena at hand. It asks why and how the members of the first Christian community came to believe and act as they did, only insofar as these questions throw light on why and how modern men and women come to believe and act as they do.[13]

The modern Christian neophyte, child or adult, confronts a world of organized religion, with its buildings, social institutions, sacred texts, creedal statements, moral norms, authority figures, canonized heroes and heroines, and a bewildering fabric of sacramental practices (e.g., devotions, fasting) and artifacts (images, the rosary, etc.). They constitute the symbol system that embodies the Church's meanings and values, expresses its attitudes and priorities and, taken together, give it identity. In other words, the modern Christian finds a world already externalized by previous generations who shared a common faith. The modern Christian comes to know it as an objectified world of structured meanings and patterned behaviors that he/she is expected to internalize.

Social scientists, students of world religions and, under the influence of the previously named groups, Christian theologians have come to make a distinction between faith and beliefs. Faith is understood as a basic orientation, a fundamental attitude, described by David Tracy as "primal and often non-conceptual."[14] It is an act of the whole person; it engages the totality of one's being, conscious and unconscious. When communities reflect upon and attempt to express faith—their belief stance vis-à-vis the transcendent, the numinous or limit situations—in concrete terms, they fall back on a variety of verbal and nonverbal symbols. In this framework beliefs are symbols that explicate particular historical, moral, or cognitive claims implicit in a particular faith stance. Religious beliefs are thematized in doctrines, moral codes, rituals, prayer formulas, and countless other commonly shared symbols. They interpret the way individuals and communities apprehend transcendent reality and at the same time provide purpose and patterns for organizing the realities of everyday living. Beliefs disclose the meanings and values implicit in the primal faith of particular communities and their members. Beliefs, grounded as they are in faith values, identify the good and evil. Faith is the primal orientation of individuals and communities in their living and feeling; specific beliefs mediate its meaning. To be socialized into a particular religious tradition, therefore, is more a matter of belief than faith.

Beliefs are expressed in symbols that explicate faith and

bring it to consciousness. There are foundational symbols and second-order symbols. For Roman Catholics (and probably for all Christians), examples of foundational symbols are Jesus Christ, Church, Eucharist, and Scripture. Second level-symbols can be as diverse as Canon Law and the parish church, the Vatican and religious orders, Gregorian chant and infant baptism. Though a specific symbol may be peculiar to Catholic practice—the rosary, for example—it does not have a religious meaning apart from the whole system wherein certain moments (mysteries) in Christ's life are understood to have special significance and Mary is accorded a singular place. The pope is another distinctively Catholic symbol. The unique authority associated with the papacy, however, can be understood only in the broader context of ecclesiology. Roman Catholics and Anglo-Catholics thus see the role of the pope in the church in a different light because they see church structure in a different light. The Roman Catholic takes his/her identity from the network of interlocking and mutually supportive beliefs, values, attitudes, and patterns of behavior that distinguishes that particular Christian tradition.

"Education in Faith"

"Faith," says John Westerhoff, "cannot be taught by any method of instruction; we can only teach religion."[15] Richard McBrien seems to agree that faith cannot be taught. "When all is said and done," he writes, "religious educators, bishops, preachers, and the Church at large do not transmit 'the faith.' They transmit particular interpretations or understandings of faith. In direct words: they transmit theologies."[16] Catechesis, which is here taken to be synonymous with "education in faith," assumes much the same thing. Faith is at once a gift of grace and the free response of the person to God's call. Because it is a grace, no human expedient can pretend to instill and increase faith, and even less to program its growth and development from the outside. "Catechetical training," in the words of Vatican II, "is intended to make men's faith become living, conscious, and active, through the light of instruction."[17] Catechesis cannot engender faith, but only awaken, nourish, and develop what is already there.

Catechesis begins as an exercise in hermeneutics. Education in faith becomes a lesson in interpreting one's personal experiences as well as historical events in the light of faith—*lumen fidei*. "There are not two sorts of human experiences," writes Peter Hebblethwaite, "one Christian and the other secularist. There is only one reality called human experience, but there are two different interpretations of it."[18] Simply to reflect, therefore, on one's own experience, to narrate historical incidents, or even to discuss current events in which the Church is involved is not enough. Catechesis is a matter of consciousness-raising, of uncovering the mysteries hidden beneath the surface of everyday life. It is an introduction to reading and interpreting signs—"the signs of the times," biblical signs, ecclesial signs (creedal symbols and life-styles), and liturgical signs. "Faith," says Karl Rahner, "is never awakened by someone having something communicated to him purely from the outside, addressed solely to his naked understanding as such. . . ." Education in faith—catechesis—therefore means "to assist understanding of what has already been experienced in the depth of human reality as grace (i.e., as in absolutely direct relation to God."[19]

The success of catechesis, therefore, is not judged by how much information, even information about religion and church, that one imbibes. Catechesis aims rather at transmitting the wisdom of a particular religious tradition, which in the context of these discussions is Roman Catholic Christianity. The so-called "experiential" and "anthropological" approaches in catechesis try to build and reinforce this heritage by integrating religion with everyday life. It is not a question of whether secular films, profane literature, popular songs, or commercial advertising have a place in the religious studies curriculum; the question is whether they are viewed, read, listened and reacted to from a distinctive point of view. How are the experiences interpreted? Value clarification and the examination of human relationships —friendship, love, sexuality—should be looked at differently in a social science program than in a religion course. It is not enough for catechists to interpret human experience in the context of a vague kind of theistic humanism that too often is passed off as "incarnational faith." Catechesis must rather present the kind of sacramental view of the universe that Langdon Gilkey and others identify as distinctively Catholic: all reality—even sin and failure—is seen as the sign and instrument of salvation.[20] The catechist has no arcane set of special truths not otherwise available, but he/she is the heir to a symbol system that has the power to disclose ultimate meaning and transform the lives of individuals and communities. (The disclosure of ultimate meaning, it should be noted, is not the same as having "all the answers.") In the final analysis, however, it is Jesus Christ, the Master Symbol—the *Ursakrament*—who reveals the mystery of salvation and sheds light on all the lesser symbols.

In the framework of the socialization model, education in the faith has three objectives. They roughly parallel the focal interests of the psychologists, the sociologists, and the anthropologists in their employment of the socialization model. The objectives may be summarized under the headings: (1) growth in personal faith; (2) religious affiliation; and (3) the maintenance and transmission of a religious tradition. In the abstract the three nicely complement one another. In the concrete, however, they are at times the source of tension. Some religious educators build programs to achieve one of the objectives, only to find that there are others in the community who would emphasize another. For purpose of analysis we proceed from the more general to the particular, and, therefore, consider the three objectives in reverse order to their listing here.

Handing on the Symbols of Faith

The Christian community believes it has a message of lasting importance. Like every group that takes itself seriously, Christians believe they have a mission to transmit this message to successive generations. Or in the language of socialization, the Christian community believes it has a responsibility to impress its institutionalized meanings and values powerfully and unforgettably on its members. It knows it cannot engender a basic faith stance, but it leads its members—potentially "all nations"—to adopt its symbols and internalize their meanings.

From Saint Paul to the present every formal effort in religious education in the history of the Church has been in one way or another an exposition of Christian symbols. Although the Christians of the early Church did not have a social science vocabulary, they were in fact consciously "socializing" their members. The catechumenate tested the moral behavior of the proselytes and gradually initiated them into the life of the community. Step by step they were introduced to the sacred texts. Though it referred primarily to the creed, the catechesis in the ancient Church peaked in a special ceremony known as the *traditio symboli*—a ritualized handing on of the symbol of faith. The catechumens who were judged "competent" for full-fledged membership were formally inducted in the baptismal rites and admitted to the eucharistic celebration. While converts from the mystery religions easily understood many of the symbolic rituals, it was necessary to make them familiar with the idiom of the Old Testament. Even the proselytes who came via Judaism had to study the particular interpretation that Christians bring to the Hebrew Scriptures. Cyril of Jerusalem, Ambrose, and Augustine have left us examples of catechetical homilies showing that they continued to explain baptism and the Eucharist even after the neophytes were received into the Church. The meaning of the Christian ritual and creed statements was no more immediately relevant to the Christians of the 4th and 5th centuries than it is to their descendants in the 20th—perhaps less so. Formal instruction played an important part, but only a part, in the socialization process.

It is obvious that our Christian understandings rest not on our individual experiences alone. Judgments by which we assent to truths of fact and value are seldom, if ever, made independently of the human community in which we find ourselves. Community assumes expression and communication. The world in which one lives is constituted of objects and ideas, patterns of behavior and social structures, verbal and nonverbal language. In the best of times, this objective reality is expressed in a coherent symbol system that yields meaning and purpose. The meaning is not always self-evident, at least to succeeding generations, and therefore needs to be mediated by stories (myths), art, ritual, and theology. In a world constituted of a number of cultures, the symbol system within a religious tradition or the symbol systems of several traditions may conflict and compete with one another. In times of rapid change and cultural upheaval, the resulting chaos and confusion are such that everything seems to lose meaning, nothing appears to have purpose, and all communication is lost.

Catechesis, therefore, has a second task: It is a matter of "world maintenance," the holding together of a shared vision of reality that gives both the community as a whole and the persons who constitute it a sense of identity. (This use of "sense" is adapted from Erikson. The patterns of identity he describes are not able to be objectified by the subject as "knowledge." Rather, he/she comes to a "sense" of who he/she is and tests it in the social and cultural context to see if it is valid.) In biblical terms, "world maintenance" is a matter of adhering to the covenant, with all that it implies for the institutional religion of the poeple of God as well as the religious individuals who make it up. Education in the faith implies, therefore, an effort to sustain the framework of meaning and value that aids communities and their members to interpret human existence and pattern their behavior.

Religious Belonging

The document *To Teach as Jesus Did*, published by the United States bishops, says that one of the goals of Catholic religious education is "to build community."[21] According to the Canon Law of the Catholic Church (and the same is more or less true for all the mainline churches), every baptized person belongs to the Church (cf. can. 87). Neither juridical membership on the one hand, nor a vague sense of belonging on the other, however, is sufficient basis to establish a community. "To build community" means in this context to socialize the members into an ecclesial community with at least minimal structures and organization.

The model here is Ferdinand Tonnies's *Gemeinschaft*. One is born into the community and accepts it as part of the external order. The archetype is family where people grow up and develop in reliance on one another. The communal bonds are inseparable from their sense of personal identity. The members of the community speak of themselves as "we," and, more or less willingly, accept the social roles that it assigns to them.[22] The primary symbol of this community, at least in the Catholic tradition, is the eucharistic assembly, Inasmuch as the Eucharist brings together the many human differences found within the boundaries of the local community and draws them into the universality of the Church, the Eucharist exemplifies both unity and catholicity. Inasmuch as it is the sacrament of Christ's passover from death to life, "where natural elements refined by man are changed into his glorified body, providing a meal of brotherly solidarity and a foretaste of the heavenly banquet," it is a sign of holiness (*Gaudium et Spes*, No. 38).

Community in this sense possesses a definite structure and implies a good deal more than a mere "collectivity of people." (It is in this latter sense that Andrew Greeley uses the term when speaking of "communal Catholics." The "Catholic community" is understood in a way roughly equivalent to the "Jewish community" or the "black community.")[23] In this context "religious belonging" becomes the fundamental relationship of a member to his or her group and implies considerably more than looking to one's roots as a source of religious attitudes and cultural outlooks. The conscious identification of a Christian with an organized church "is no longer a fact viewed from the exterior, a fact reported to a census taker, or a religious category; it is a psychological reality."[24] The member sees him/herself in interaction with the group. The group, for its part, welcomes and motivates the member; he/she participates in its activities and is concerned with its well-being and governance.

In the framework of a faith community, catechesis becomes community education. It consists of a fragile network of interlocking and mutually supportive institutions and agencies, professional leaders and private citizens, formal and informal influences, through which a person comes to identify with the Church. It begins with the human community, the family, the neighborhood, perhaps the ethnic tradition of a people like the Irish, Italians, or the Poles whose history was closely bound with the fortunes of Catholicism. The home nurtures the basic aspirations and attitudes of children and adults alike through the very atmosphere that prevails there. The presence of religious art, a Bible, a crucifix, religious periodicals, and so forth, is an informal way of transmitting the traditional symbols of Catholicism. The very image of the parish church in the eyes of the individuals and the families that constitute it projects an ecclesiology: Is it the image of a building that may be rented for weddings and funerals, a refuge where one may find a moment of peace and quiet away from the pressures of urban life, a place of common prayer and meaningful worship, a center of social action? All or none of the foregoing? The parochial school is an influential instrument of socialization not only for what it teaches in a formal way but also for what it teaches indirectly and in passing. A very effective social justice curriculum may be offset by the unspoken reality that the church school in fact flourishes as an escape from racial integration. Then there is the observance of Sundays and the celebration of the liturgical cycles with the advent and lenten rituals culminating in Christmas and Easter. The attitudes and priorities manifested in the patterns of belief and behavior in a local Christian community have a more lasting effect than formal instruction. A parish congregation that self-consciously strives to be truly one, holy, catholic, and apostolic leaves its mark on every other socializing agent it comes into contact with.

The recent document, *A Vision of Youth Ministry*, published by the United States Catholic Conference, outlines a program of community education for young people. The many and varied facets of this ministry are brought into focus by a common dedication to two main goals: (1) the "personal and spiritual growth of each young person," and (2) "responsible participation in the life, mission and work of the faith community."[25] It is the latter goal that is of interest at this moment. The document sees catechesis primarily as a form of the ministry of the word, but it recognizes that it is integral to and in practice inseparable from the ministries of healing, enabling, guidance, worship, and service. The strategies whether in schools of one kind or another or in less-structured educational settings are designed "to draw young people into the supportive experience of Christian community, and to assist the parish community to welcome the young and share its ministry with them."[26]

"Community," according to *To Teach as Jesus Did*, "is at the heart of Christian education not simply as a concept to be taught but as a reality to be lived" (No. 23). The young are socialized through an interaction with the adult community that witnesses to faith and provides role models for youth to imitate and emulate. They acquire a religious identity by taking as their own the creedal formulas, rites, the activities and other emblems that symbolize the corporate solidarity of the Catholic community. "For the early adolescent," says John Nelson of Fordham University, "doctrine serves not so much as a formulation of truth as it does a symbol of orthodoxy within a religious group."[27] Even before the meanings of the symbols are internalized, and before they are seen as an organic whole—as a system—the young Christian as it were wears them as badges of belonging.

But not only adolescents are brought to faith through socialization nor does the process stop in adulthood. The renewed catechumenate, for example, advocated by the recently promulgated *Rite of Christian Initiation of Adults*, operates from the same premise. Aidan Kavanagh argues that it offers a paradigm for the radical renewal of all Christian life. The new rite, he says, "*re*-unites (italics mine) a complex and long-term process of human formation with ritual-sacramental engagement in a robust ecclesial environment."[28] The modernized catechumenate provides another example of socialization in which the process and ritual of Christian formation create the faith community, sustain and at times modify it, and keep the community a functioning entity. The ultimate success of the socialization process, therefore, must be judged in terms not of how many children or even converts are baptized, but rather by answering how well adults are assimilated into the faith community and how closely they identify with it. It is on this premise that the General Catechetical Directory states:

> Catechesis for adults, since it deals with persons who are capable of an adherence that is fully responsible, must be considered the chief form of catechesis. All the other forms, which are indeed always necessary, are in some way oriented to it (No. 20).

Personal Faith
Even though faith is nurtured in the faith community—in the

Church as the Pentecostal assembly—it is, nonetheless, a personal grace. Contemporary theologians speak of it as a personal encounter with God in that faith represents an individual's response to the word of God in Jesus Christ. The encounter is described as personal because it involves one's whole being —entire person—mind, heart, and soul. Faith has a cognitive or intellectual dimension, but it is more than knowing something about God; it is knowing God. Faith implies loving, valuing, caring, and feeling as well.

Catechesis thus seeks to address the whole person. It recognizes the uniqueness of every individual and, therefore, suspects any structures that would indoctrinate and hinder the inner growth of a deep personal relationship with God. Education in faith respects the freedom of the person and, therefore, resists any pressures that try to force a response. Education in faith focuses on individual needs and, therefore, in every case observes the person's natural disposition, ability, age, and circumstances of life.

The *General Catechetical Directory* recognizes that children, adolescents, young adults, and mature grown-ups have different needs and dispositions. It sketches, in broad outline, principles and concerns that should guide catechesis according to age levels. The description is purposefully unsophisticated, but the *GCD* does emphasize that "the life of faith passes through various stages, just as does man's existence while he is attaining maturity and taking on the duties of life" (No. 30; cf. Part V). It admits, moreover, that stage-development allows for various degrees "both in the global acceptance of the total word of God and in the explanation of that word and the application of it to the different duties of human life, according to the maturity of each and differences of individuals" (ibid).

It is now commonplace to hear theologians speak of doctrinal development, and moralists discuss the development of conscience, and psychologists describe cognitive development, but it is a relatively new phenomenon to hear religious educators talking about faith development. Until recently, few recognized the importance of the personal dynamic in the structure of faith. It is not merely that the creedal formula takes on new meanings because of doctrinal development, but the person professing the creed is also subject to change. It is largely due to the work of James W. Fowler III, whose "structuralist-developmental" approach is now well known, that religious educators have become sensitive to this aspect of faith development.

Fowler's research is particularly helpful, moreover, in understanding catechesis as a dimension of the socialization process. He acknowledges his indebtedness to Jean Piaget, Lawrence Kohlberg, and Erik Erikson among others. All three in various ways argue that an individual internalizes patterns of knowing and behavior through his/her interaction with objects and persons. Development comes through a person's efforts to accomodate oneself to one's environment.

Beginning with the premise that faith is a kind of knowing, Fowler has undertaken to adapt the research techniques of Piaget and Kohlberg to the area of "faith-knowing." "Faith," he writes, "is a knowing which includes loving, caring and valuing, as well as awe, dread and fear. Faith-knowing relates a person or community to the limiting boundaries and depths of experience; to the source, center and standard of valuing or responsibility in life."[29] In short, faith presents a set of operations in which cognition and affection are inextricably entwined. Just as Piaget had only a secondary interest in a child's knowledge of mathematics, physics, and logic, and just as Kohlberg's primary interest is not in the outcomes of moral decisions for their own sake, so Fowler does not focus on the content of faith as such. In fact, he has found that "the same or similar content of faith may be appropriated in quite different ways by persons whose faith-knowing is structurally different at different stages." Fowler, however, acknowledges a special difficulty in his research "due to the fact that the dimension of experience we refer to as God or the Transcendent must be symbolically represented and mediated in ways which the parties to moral conflict need not necessarily be."[30]

Taking the six stages of moral development identified by Kohlberg as a starting point, Fowler subsequently modified them in the light of his own research. On the basis of several hundred in-depth interviews conducted with persons of various ages and background, he developed a taxonomy of operations or structures in faith-knowing. Each of the six stages has its own particular wholeness, set of operations, and particular competencies. A brief outline of the stages is given here only to illumine how growth in faith is inextricably wound up with socialization. The reader must go directly to Fowler's own writings for a fuller and properly nuanced description.

Stage I: Intuitive-Projective Faith. The child is powerfully influenced by the examples, moods, actions, and language of the visible faith of significant adults. The phase is characterized by imitation. There is little distinction between fact and fantasy.

Stage II: Mythic-Literal Faith. The person begins to appropriate the stories, beliefs, and rituals that symbolize one's identity with a faith community. Concepts tend to be largely concrete in reference; symbols, one-dimensional and literal. Mythic forms function in lieu of explanation. Appeal to trusted authority (parents rather than peers) serves as the basis for verification.

Stage III: Synthetic-Conventional Faith. Faith is required to help provide a coherent and meaningful synthesis of involvements that grow increasingly complex and diverse and extend beyond the family. The individual, however, does not yet have to make a personal synthesis of meaning. The conventional wisdom suffices.

Stage IV: Individuating-Reflexive Faith. This stage marks the collapse of the kind of synthesis adequate in previous stages. The responsibility for a world synthesis and particular life-style shifts more clearly to the individual. Faith is called upon to help reduce the tension between such unavoidable polarities as individuality versus belonging to community, self-fulfillment versus service to others, the relative versus the absolute, and so forth. A person in Stage IV is likely "to see most institutional religion as 'conventional' and to be drawn to the exotic or novel in traditions."[31]

Stage V: Paradoxical-Consolidative Faith. Authority has been fully internalized. "Faith-knowing involves, at this stage, a moral or volitional affirmation of that which is somewhat paradoxical; it affirms the beliefs, symbols and rituals of a community while 'seeing through' them in a double sense. It sees the relativity, partiality, and time-boundness of the tradition—the scandal of its particularity. But it also sees and values it as a way to see through to the Universal it mediates. What Stage V sees in its own faith-knowing and its symbols, rituals and the like, it also acknowledges in the developed traditions of other persons and cultures. Stage V generally involves a reappropriation (and reinterpretation) of one's past, and of the significant persons and groups whose example and teachings influence its growth in faith-knowing."[32]

Stage VI: Universalizing Faith. Few reach this stage. It is characterized "by an integration of life in faith in which immediacy of participation in the Ultimate is the fruit of development, of discipline, and, likely, of genius."[33] The sense of the oneness of all persons becomes a permeative basis for decision and action. Particulars are cherished because they are vessels of the universal. Life is both loved and held loosely.

It is not necessary, however, to discuss all the related issues to establish the usefulness of the stage-theory advanced by Fowler. Catechetics has long needed a paradigm like the stages of faith-knowing to help explain what it means when it says, as the *General Catechetical Directory* and other contemporary works repeatedly do, that the goal of catechesis is "maturity of faith."

Personal faith is caught up in the dynamic of human development. Growth in faith implies ongoing conversion, a gradual transformation of consciousness. Conversion brings individuals (and, though it is not to the point here, communities) to a new awareness of themselves and a fresh orientation to the world around them. It is in this sense that conversion is a principal goal of catechesis. Conversion implies a shift or at least a broadening of one's horizons; and it implies self-transcendence. Bernard Lonergan distinguishes three types of conversion: intellectual, moral, and religious. Since each of the three is connected with the other two, the goal of catechesis comprises them all while being primarily concerned with religious conversion.

Intellectual conversion is a broadening of one's perceptual horizon so that the individual recognizes the world of mediated meaning to be no less real than the world of immediacy. The world of immediacy, the horizon of the child and the empiricist, in Lonergan's categories is the sum of what is seen, heard, touched, tasted, smelled, felt. The world of meaning is "not known by the sense experience of an individual but by the external and internal experience of a cultural community."[34]

Moral conversion changes one's horizons so that one's choice and decisions are made not on the basis of personal gratification but on a basis of values. The person arrives at a point where he/she discovers that choosing affects oneself no less than the objects chosen or rejected. It is a step toward authenticity and becoming "inner directed." In sum, moral conversion, writes Lonergan, "consists in opting for the truly good, even for value against satisfaction when value and satisfaction conflict."[35]

Religious conversion represents a shift in one's ground of being. It is a change from temporal and transitory, particular and personal, interests to a more efficacious ground for the pursuit of intellectual and moral ends. "Religious conversion," says Lonergan, "is being grasped by ultimate concern."[36] Truth and moral goodness imply holiness, but religious conversion adds a distinct quality of its own. It is a total being-in-love; it is other-worldly fulfillment.

Conversion and catechesis are so inextricably linked that they serve to define each other.[37] They work together reinterpreting one's past biography, and checking and rechecking one's judgments and understandings against the judgments and understandings of the community. The transformation of consciousness builds on primary internalizations and, except in those "first conversions" that represent an about-face and radical repudiation of everything that went before, generally avoids abrupt discontinuity with subjective biography of the individual.[38] Conversion and catechesis within the context of the faith community do not necessitate a total resocialization so much as they imply that socialization is a continuing process through life. As long as the process is not fixated at some point in one's development it will result in maturity of faith.

Maturity of faith no longer appears as a static point one may or may not reach in adult years. That faith is a dynamic element in the life of individuals and the community is not an entirely new discovery. The New Testament uses a variety of images to make this point. One must struggle to preserve, cultivate, and bring faith to maturity. Maturity of faith is experienced at each stage when individuals—children, adolescents, adults—harmoniously integrate faith-knowing with other operational structures in the overall patterns of psychological development, cognitional and affective. Each stage is characterized by a delicate equilibrium that has its own comprehensiveness and potential integrity. When this balance is achieved by a child according to his or her years or by an adult in a primitive culture, one can properly speak of maturity of faith. Even though Fowler's descriptions are said to be provisional, they can be most helpful in setting objectives and planning strategies for various groups who are being catechized. They bring the theology of grace and the process of socialization, which too frequently move in different orbits, into dialogue with each other.

III. Implications

The point of departure for this paper and (as I understand it) one of the underlying premises of this dialogue is the need to clarify the purpose, nature, and task of religious education. It is only when an agent, whether an institution or an individual, has a clear grasp of the overall context in which it functions that the significance of particular strategies and tactics can be judged. It is the thesis of this paper that the socialization model provides (1) a heuristic tool for a better understanding of what much of religious education is about, and (2) a clearly defined basis for planning programs.

Insofar as religious education is a socialization process, I refer to it as catechesis. The term, hallowed by tradition (which has caused some to disdain it as "archaic"),[39] embodies the threefold goal of religious education that has concerned the Christian community from New Testament times: (1) the broadening of one's horizons—growth in personal faith, (2) the gradual incorporation of members into a society of believers—religious belonging, and (3) the maintenance and transmission of a particular symbol system that constitutes and expresses Catholic identity—communicating meaning. Although education in faith is related to religious instruction, religious formation, and other dynamics that are part of all religious education, its purpose is at once consciously both personal and communal. Whatever the means used in catechesis, they are seen as tactics in the broader strategy of socialization that ideally leads to maturity of faith.

A number of practical implications flow from viewing religious education as socialization. This is not to say that sacramental preparation, Bible study, human experience, social action, and similar activities are ignored in other models of religious education, but it does suggest that they play a different role and have a different significance in catechesis. Without going into great detail, I mention in closing only a few of the more obvious implications implicit in the socialization model.

1. The socialization model opens the way for a stronger emphasis in religious education on process. This is not to say that methodology assumes the chief role, but rather it is an honest acknowledgement that catechesis in the final analysis is community education. The community of faith with all its formal and informal structures is the chief catechist. Professionals and paraprofessionals engaged in various aspects of the educational ministry are its agents.

2. A corollary of the above is that catechesis not merely with individuals but with the community taken as a whole. The socialization process implies the transformation (though I have not emphasized this aspect in these pages) as well as the transmission of culture. Just as the individual Christian needs to undergo continuous conversion, so too must the Christian community constantly broaden its horizons, reforming and renewing itself. Catechists thus become agents of change.

3. The content of religious education is not "faith" as a kind of abstraction. It is always mediated by a symbol system. The teaching of doctrine becomes a means—albeit one of the most important, only a means—in communicating meaning and giving the community a sense of identity. Religious language—myths, parables, and other narratives—and theology are other means of transmitting the symbols of faith. The success or failure of catechetical programs must ultimately be judged in terms of how effectively the socialization process is proceeding, not in terms of how much information church members have.

4. Unlike theology, which (from a catechetical viewpoint) is a means, ritual and liturgy are part and parcel of community

experience. Like all experience they have an educational dimension, but the sacramental liturgy is to be celebrated for its own ends, not merely for its educational purpose.

5. Ultimately, the success of the socialization process is judged in terms of the adult members of the community: how well they understand and carry on the mission of Christ in the world, the mission the Church has assumed as its own.

Notes

1. M. Sawick and B. L. Marthaler, eds., "Symposium on the Catechesis of Children and Youth" (Papers from the Symposium, Marriottsville, Md., March 13-16, 1977; to be published later in 1977).

2. Cf. I. Ramsey, *Models and Mystery* (Oxford: Oxford Univ. Press, 1964); I.G. Barbour, *Myths, Models and Paradigms* (New York: Harper & Row, 1974). The world of science identifies several kinds of models that serve different functions. The model attempted here might best be described in Barbour's terms as a "theoretical model." It is "an imagined mechanism or process, postulated by *analogy* with familiar mechanisms or processes and used to construct a *theory* to correlate a set of observations" (p. 30). In this sense modeling is an intermediate stage in Lonergan's modes of consciousness between the realm of common sense and the realm of theory, a necessary step as one moves from the world of immediacy into a world mediated by meaning (Cf. Bernard Lonergan, *Method in Theology* [New York: Herder & Herder, 1972], pp. 81-90).

3. The above introduction to socialization draws heavily on Clausen's essay "A Historical and Comparative View of Socialization Theory and Research," in *Socialization and Society*, J. A. Clausen, ed. (Boston: Little, Brown and Co., 1964). Cf. also K. Danzinger, *Socialization* (Baltimore: Penguin Books, 1971).

4. H. P. Dreitzel, ed., *Childhood and Socialization*, Recent Sociology 5 (New York: Macmillan, 1973), p. 6.

5. Clausen, *Socialization and Society*, p. 31.

6. P.L. Berger and Thomas Luckmann, *The Social Construction of Reality* (New York: Anchor Books, 1967), p. 78.

7. Ibid., p. 61. Cf. D.M. Rafky, "Phenomenology and Socialization: Some Comments on the Assumptions Underlying Socialization Theory," in Dreitzel, *Childhood and Socialization*, pp. 44-64.

8. Berger and Luckmann, *The Social Construction of Reality*, p. 9.

9. G. Baum, in *The Ecumenist*, March-April 1971, p. 43.

10. Berger and Luckmann, *The Social Construction of Reality*, p. 131.

11. The quote is from Baum's article in *The Ecumenist* (see n. 9 above), but he says much the same in his Foreword to A. Greeley, *The New Agenda* (Garden City, N.Y.: Image Books, 1975), and in his own *Religion and Alienation* (New York: Paulist Press, 1975), pp. 238-265.

12. For an extensive analysis of the nature and task of catechesis, cf. A. Exeler, *Wesen und Aufgabe der Katechese* (Freiburg im Breisgau: Herder, 1966). Exeler offers a lengthy excursus on the history of the term *catechein* (pp. 223-232), and a survey of catechesis—its specific function—in the life of the Church (pp. 256-276).

13. It should be noted, however, that "Christianity itself starts as a community of believers, united by their faith in the resurrection of Christ and living in shared expectation of that eschatological fulfillment which is described as the 'heavenly Jerusalem.' It is not difficult to assemble New Testament texts that point to the fostering of Christian community as the goal towards which are directed the behavior of Christians, the efforts of the specialized ministry, and the redeeming action of Christ himself in his Spirit" (B. Cooke, *Ministry to Word and Sacraments* [Philadelphia: Fortress Press, 1976], p. 35).

14. David Tracy, *Blessed Rage for Order* (New York: Seabury Press, 1975), p. 16, n. 13.

15. John Westerhoff, *Will Our Children Have Faith?* (New York: Seabury Press, 1976), p. 23.

16. Richard McBrien, "Faith, Theology and Belief," *Commonweal*, November 15, 1974.

17. *Christus Dominus* ("The Bishops' Pastoral Office in the Church"), p. 14.

18. Peter Hebblethwaite, "Man's Search for Meaning," *The Month*, May 1976, p. 163.

19. *Sacramentum Mundi* 2:311.

20. Langdon Gilkey, *Catholicism Confronts Modernity* (New York: Seabury Press, 1975).

21. See n. 17 above.

22. Cf. G. Baum, *Religion and Alienation*, pp. 45-67. Also J. J. Dewitt, *Making a Community Out of a Parish* (Washington: The Liturgical Conference, 1966).

23. Andrew Greeley, *The Communal Catholic* (New York: Seabury Press, 1976), pp. 3, 10-11.

24. H. Carrier, *The Sociology of Religious Belonging* (New York: Herder and Herder), p. 58.

25. *A Vision of Youth Ministry* (Washington, D.C.: U.S. Catholic Conference, Dept. of Education, 1976), p. 4.

26. Ibid.

27. From an unpublished paper delivered at a "Symposium on the

Catechesis of Children and Youth," cf. n. 1 above.

28. Aidan Kavanagh, "Adult Initiation: Process and Ritual," *Liturgy: Journal of the Liturgical Conference*, January 1977, p. 7 (italics mine).

29. James W. Fowler, "Towards a Developmental Perspective on Faith," *Religious Education* 69 (March-April 1974), 211.

30. Ibid., p. 213.

31. Ibid., p. 217.

32. Ibid.

33. "Stages of Faith" (A report submitted to a symposium at Fordham University, September 1975), p. 33.

34. Lonergan, *Method*, p. 238.

35. Ibid., p. 240.

36. Ibid.

37. F. Coudreau, *Basic Catechetical Perspectives* (New York: Paulist Press, 1970), p. 30.

38. Cf. Berger and Luckmann, *The Social Construction of Reality*, p. 161.

39. E.G. Lee and J.M. Lee, *The Religious Education We need* (Mishawaka, Ind.: Religious Education Press, 1977), p. 4.

Where Now, What Next

GABRIEL MORAN

We are asked to define religious education. The question appears to be a simple one even if there are expected disagreements in the answer. But I prefer to step back from that question and spend what may seem an inordinate amount of space examining the nature of the question. What does it mean to define any term? I remember reading as a college freshman William James's statement that all the great philosophical questions are arguments over words. I thought then that James was ridiculous but now I think I understand him. He didn't mean that philosophical (and religious) differences are pseudo-problems that can be cleared up by people's getting the "right" definitions. He meant that progress in human discourse is one of constantly attending to the meaning(s) of the words.

As a start I would distinguish between a descriptive definition and an advocative definition. In the former, one gives the actual and operative meaning of a term (a difficult and ambitious job in itself). In the latter, one advocates what the meaning of the term should be (which raises questions about the criteria of the advocated meaning). Very often in arguments one person is using a word to describe, the other person is using it to advocate. One might say (depending on your definition) that they are not arguing at all. W. C. Smith has pointed out that in religious arguments one person usually argues from the real condition of the opponent's religion and the ideal (or advocated) condition of his/her own religion.[1] Both are asserting the truth: Both suspect that their opponent is dishonest. Church members are vulnerable to a charge of deceit when they say "A Christian is one who . . ." What follows may be a description of something that has never existed. The problem is not so much deceit as a compound confusion over the use of language and the advocacy of change.

A descriptive definition attempts to state how a term is currently used. That meaning, of course, differs according to place, social class, and so forth. Old and rich words are (by definition) highly ambiguous. How does one find the meaning of a term? Etymology and history are always a help though they don't settle the matter. One looks at how the word is being used by people or institutions one considers significant. There is no closure on this process, which is why the advocative definition is both possible and necessary. As one describes, one is consciously or not choosing what is significant (or preferable) from almost unlimited data.

Human life gets along ordinarily because there is an overlapping of meaning when people use the few thousand words that constitute most speech. People can't get full agreement on what they mean but they can largely agree on what they *don't* mean. That is, it is helpful in defining to say what the term does not mean. That step helps to uncover the classificatory system in which the term operates. For example, if one studies the use of "religious education" in churches (its main operative setting), one finds that it is completely opposed to many things one might *logically* suppose were religious, educational, or both. A parish board, say, may have a school committee and a religious education committee.

The advocative meaning must in some way be latent in the operative meaning. In advocating, one is trying to recover or discover a realm of meaning that has been obscured by a dominant meaning. One can advocate that almost any word means almost anything. Obviously it helps to know some etymology and history. It is also important to have "demonstration groups" who exemplify the advocated meaning.

The power to classify is enormous. Once the system of categories defining an institution is established, the speech within that institution does little to control the workings of the institution. The most frightening thing in the 20th century is the unimaginable size of some institutions. The danger is not that their intentions are evil; rather, their power to classify and thereby control will corrupt unless there are counterforces. The difficulty is in finding social/institutional leverage to provide criticism of ABC/

CBS/NBC, *Time/Newsweek/New York Times*, American/Soviet/Chinese, Exxon/GM/IBM. Before churches and universities rush in to provide the answer, they need first to explore how deeply they are part of the problem.

By insisting on distinctions of language I am trying to avoid the posture of attacking institutions in the name of individual liberty. Language is a social reality and examining language is a way to overcome divisions among persons, groups, and institutions. For example, instead of attacking "the church" I think it is preferable to distinguish church from church official, church official from church office, etc. Descriptively, church usually does mean church official but there is good basis for distinguishing what church could mean from what it does mean. The term "institutional church" is presumably trying to get at this problem but its effect is perverse and misleading. The implication is that there is a "non-institutional church" and this assumption allows critics to pretend that they are not part of the problem. Interestingly, the phrase "institutional church" was coined in the late 19th century to refer to churches deeply involved in social services.[2] The term was simply misleading then but it is now a serious obstacle to accepting the operative meaning of church and advocating a change of meaning.

Let me cite one example at length. Actually it is more than an example because everything I have written in religious education depends on this definition. Since the first article I ever wrote I have waged a battle for the meaning of "intelligence." I have advocated a meaning that goes against the operative one. I base my advocacy on etymology, history, some current usage, and the urgent need to have a word for the greatest of human activity/receptivity. I have always distinguished intelligent from rational so that intelligent is both rational and nonrational. I thereby give over the word "rational" to its currently established meaning (the movement from premise to conclusion by the capacity to think and to control data). There are writers today who try to make a distinction *within* reason (e.g., technical vs. substantial). I doubt they will be any more successful than M. B. Eddy's (and others') attempt to define the *real* meaning of science in the late 19th century.[3]

When I started writing I carefully stated my meaning of intelligence. I was naive enough to think that my meaning would be understood. I was dumbfounded, therefore, when I was accused of "rationalism" or of not being interested in "emotion." I had said that intelligence is not reducible to reason; I had said my meaning of intelligence includes feeling. Why would people not hear that? The answer is obvious to me now. The meaning of the word is set by assumptions in the culture and powerful institutions. Why then bother to fight? Because to get a serious hearing for religious education (and philosophy and much else in life) one needs either the distinction between reason and intelligence or some other distinction just as difficult to come by.

The reduction of the word intelligence is not a casual accident nor one correctible by a simple statement of the *real* meaning. Institutions control speech for their own purposes; the finest and richest words are the most attractive. To the extent that an institution can get the best words, the easier it is to justify itself and all its doings. The more questionable the institution's legitimacy, the greater its appetite for the best words. The word "intelligence" has rich possibilities. But two controls upon its current meaning are especially deleterious: the IQ syndrome and the military. I think that it is not an accident that these 2 disparate contexts are historically related. The IQ test got its start by tests with the military in World War I.

"Military intelligence" is not a new term but recently its presence has grown exponentially. Every day the *Times*, *Globe*, CBS, and so forth, refer to the "intelligence community," i.e., the United States system of spying. If the United States needs spies (as I think it may) they ought to be called spies or almost any other name except the "intelligence community" (the second word is as bad as the first).

The more obvious educational use of intelligence is in connection with IQ.[4] The attempt to attach one number to intelligence should have been suspect immediately. The outrageous racial and class bias of the tests should have discredited the whole project. Yet to this day the IQ is powerful. Intense arguments swirl around the work of A. R. Jensen in this country and Cyril Burt in England. People fighting racial or other bias often fight on the wrong terms. Lower scores of blacks (or in an earlier day "alpines") don't so much discredit particular groups as discredit the concept of IQ. (There may be some genuine genetic and hereditary issues at stake in this discussion but the IQ test is a diversion to intelligent search.)

The reader may protest that she/he does not think of the military or IQ when I say intelligence. True. But these two are cause and symptom of a reduced meaning of intelligence, a meaning set by scientific (and pseudoscientific) reasoning. At the center of religious education is the question: How can one be not rational and yet not irrational (a word that always connotes the bizarre and destructive)? There is no way to answer that question unless intelligence (or some other word) means the rational/nonrational in unity.

Defining Religious Education

This long introduction helps to situate the question: What is the meaning of the term religious education? I might answer that the *real* meaning (or Moran's meaning) is—and then describe some logically correct meaning of the words. This approach would probably be of little help and could even be an obstacle to facing the double question: Where are we now with the term religious education? Where can we go from here? I shall eventually propose a logically legitimate and politically feasible meaning of the term. First, one must ask how "religious education" functions in the language now.

I think the answer is fairly clear: There are 2 competing meanings whose strength depends upon the exact social setting. I think both meanings are inadequate, one reason being that they are ecclesiastically determined. Note I don't say it is a discussion intramural to church; even people who want nothing to do with the church speak a language determined by the church in the United States (one would have to follow a different course in other countries). The people who now take a positive interest in this question are usually church people but other people can be very interested when they see that the discussion affects them.

There is one stream in which religious education is a somewhat fuzzy and generalized term. It is traceable to what was called "liberal theology." One might call it an "extra-denominational" approach to education in religion. The Religious Education Association (REA) has reflected this wide, broad (or abstract?) meaning. The keynote speaker at its first convention was John Dewey. I mean no disparagement of either the REA or Dewey. But I think that Dewey and many others like him in his time wanted to be religious in a general way but not in any particular sense. I can certainly sympathize with that feeling but it simply won't do. Because of this connotation of "religious education" there are churches in which the term is not really operative at all.

The second strand of the current meaning of religious education is that set of activities which are designed to produce practicing church members. Here the term is an alternative to what is called "Christian education" in Protestantism and catechetics in Roman Catholicism. Both of these terms are relatively recent in their current meanings but now firmly established.

The move from liberal to neoorthodox theology was accompanied by a change from "religious education" to "Christian education." In a recent book John Westerhoff notes on page 4 that "Religious education changed its name to Christian education . . . ."[5] After that he uses the terms interchangeably and with no comment on this extraordinary fact. It would be equivalent to a political scientist's saying that in the 1940s democratic government became Americanism and now those are interchangeable terms.

In the opposite direction, Marvin Taylor has an extraordinary statement in the preface of his edited *Foundations for Christian Education in an Era of Change.*[6] He notes that a big difference from his edited collection of 10 years ago is the use of religious education rather than Christian education by the writers. However, for the purpose of symmetry in the titles, he kept Christian education. This is a supreme case of an editor's undermining what his writers are trying to say. The authors in any case would be unsuccessful in getting to "religious education" because they are nearly all Protestant. (A Catholic voice is allowed in the person of James Lee.)

From the two strands of the operative meaning I draw this

conclusion for advocacy: A more adequate meaning of religious education would be one that embraces both particular and universal. As a start, the particular must be in a context that creates tension with what is beyond itself. The best tension would be with particulars of the same kind. Even if that is not immediately possible (the co-option of language by one group may make it impossible to have particulars of the same kind) there can be a beginning purification of language. Although a developed language of religious education is not available outside of the church setting, one can refrain from speaking of religious education as a possession of the church. Not that the absence of the other is total. For example, Jewish groups exist with educational practices that are certainly not reducible to "Christian education." This other is not enough; Jewish education has many of the same structural problems as does the Christian Church(es). Religious education eventually has to include not only Jewish (and Moslem, Buddhist, etc.) education but another kind of education that cuts in a different way organizationally. Religious education has to include whole areas that are not now under any religious organization.

Religious Community

This last point relates to a conclusion I reached in the late 1960s: One cannot change "religious education" without changing the organizational form of the Christian church(es). In 1968 I coauthored a book about changing canonical religious orders/ congregations of the Roman Catholic Church. The subtitle of this book (*EIC*) is "Should Religious Life Survive?"[7] The problem is, I was accepting even while fighting the misleading usage of the words "religious life" (and "religious community," "the religious," etc.) in the Roman Catholic Church. My conceptual and linguistic failure accounts for the sarcasm in the book. However, I learned something from writing that book: One cannot change an institution while accepting uncritically its terms of self-description.

Eighteen months later I published a better book on the topic (*TRP*). It wasn't a great book but at least I had hold of the real problem, namely, the way in which the Church is categorized.

The single most important church question for me is doing away with the categories (the words) clergy/religious/lay. I emphasize I am fighting the *words*, not attacking one of these groups. The three words (or if the middle collapses, the first and third) stand and fall together. If I advocate a church without a clergy, I obviously advocate a church without a laity. I maintain that this system of classification is not an educational one and is obstructive to education.

One should note here that attempts to improve the lot of a "laity" are doomed before they start. At a recent meeting of "lay people" the *Boston Globe* quoted one woman: "It's as if we were lay people by default because we're not nuns or priests." Exactly. And by definition that's the way it will remain unless one changes the terms of the discussion (including nuns or priests in the meaning of lay or more likely by eliminating the word lay and distinguishing priest from clergyman and nun from religious). Anyone working for the "lay" in the Church should consider Freud's *The Question of Lay Analysis*. Freud was rightfully worried that the medical profession in the United States would capture psychoanalysis for the rich and powerful. Freud should have argued for a nonmedical model (and sometimes does) but being a doctor himself he couldn't extricate himself from that model. In any fight within the medical model between professional and lay, the professional wins—practically by definition.

The term "lay theology" is practically a contradiction in terms. That fact is most clear in Protestantism where "theological education" and "Christian education" are mutually exclusive in meaning. "Theological education" is used interchangeably with seminary. If seminarians take a course in "Christian education" it is not intended to give them an education that is Christian but to prepare them to deal with their (lay) educational workers. There is simply no way to propose changes in the form of Christianly religious communities while the categories of Protestant and Catholic churches remain as they are.

My original interest in "community" was my personal involvement in a Roman Catholic religious order/congregation. It slowly dawned on me that the questions of family, community, and corporation are at the center of education. Furthermore, the peculiar way that the Catholic church speaks of "community" was a key to the question. I should note that the Catholic Church is not alone here. While reading Rosabeth Kanter's fine study *Commitment and Community*[8] I realized that they don't speak that differently in the sociology department of Harvard. That is, Kanter studies the 19th-century utopian experiments but she slides into equating the word community with these peculiar experiments. Thus, normal people live in families; kooky people have communities. So it is in the history of the colonies/United States: The major chord equates family and community while the minor chord rebels and opposes family to community. I now see as central to religious education the affirmation of the family within a context of nonfamilial but communal forms of organization. The Christian Church(es) is part of the problem but it is also a possibility for working at the problem.

My writing on "religious community" provided me with a better method to analyze "religious education." Instead of working with the operative meaning assumed in the Church, I tried to advocate a new meaning (which has old roots). The obvious way to do it is to break the term into its component parts and rebuild the term. In 1970 I published a small book (*DFR*) that I hoped would spark discussion about the meaning of the words "religious education." I started by asking why religious education is neither very religious nor very educational. That is, what is called religious education in churches does not function as part of education (cf. most graduate programs). But also it is not part of a discipline of religion, especially if one notes the distinction between theology and religion (religiology).

What I tried to do in *DFR* was to sketch a curriculum for religious education. The *religious* curriculum is from birth to death (birth and death in fact being important religious moments) but the teaching/study of explicitly Christian material might be only a small part of the curriculum. Without unduly inflating the term religious education I was claiming that a family meal, the study of the social sciences, or playing basketball is already a part of religious education.

That is *not* to say that religious education is everything; therefore, religious education is nothing. There are criteria one can develop for judging whether eating and basketball are educative or miseducative. I would never underestimate the study of religion with all of the academic trappings. But I was trying to situate the *study* and the *religion* within a different meaning of *curriculum*, that is, the places we go, the people we meet, and the ways we interact with our environment.

In *DFR* I hadn't entirely broken free from the old method (as my use of "faith" or "theology" would indicate; or worse, the sexist language). The assumptions I was fighting are deeply embedded in the language and constantly reinforced. In my book *RB* I finally did get to the process of linguistic control. I consider the second chapter of that book the most important thing I have written. I examine there the use of language in the United States, especially in contemporary society dominated by the economic corporation. The three possible counterforces (education, community, religion) are allowed to exist on two conditions: They are identified with a single institution (school, family, church) and that institution is identified with minors (directed by men, staffed mainly by women, for the good of children). To the extent that the church (those who speak for that institution) accepts the identification (religion = church) then the Church reproduces the pattern of language within itself: Religious community and religious education become the names of subinstitutions that are highly praised but kept away from the center of power in the Church. To this day the operative meaning of religious education is something women do to children under the control of men.

Until one breaks this linguistic pattern, then, theorizing about religious education will probably reinforce the currently inadequate pattern of institutionalization. My book *RB* is about Church reform. Instead of using the Church to judge religious education, I use religious education (and religious community) to judge the Church. I know how silly that thesis has to sound within ecclesiastical assumptions but I think I have sufficient basis on etymology, logic, history, and contemporary forms of education and religion to stand by my criteria. I don't wish to deny the religious claims of the Christian church(es), but if one is going to engage in the fruitful activity called education, one cannot decide the outcome of the game before one starts to play.

Revelation

There is one more piece of the picture for me before I place my meaning of religious education in a conceptual model. I have found the image, idea, and word "revelation" to be a helpful tool. Both the history of the word and its near disappearance in Christian writing today is significant for religious education.

When I started studying religious education in the early 1960s the two systems I was given to work with were called theology and catechetics. At that time there didn't seem to be much interaction between them. Catechetics was trying to avoid theology and live by Scripture alone. Theology had little awareness that there was catechetics unless catechetics was defined as a minor branch of theology. I looked for a connecting image that would open exchange in both directions. The concept of revelation seemed to be what I was looking for. It was the assumption that established (and in a sense closed) theology. By opening the idea of revelation I thought theology would find the need of education not as a consequence of theology but as a context for theology's existence.

Given my intention, the title *TOR* was wholly inadequate. I was placing the word revelation within theology though I was trying to get the word revelation out from under theology's control. Having a "theology of revelation" link theology and catechetics was comparable to having B'nai B'rith mediate the Jewish-Arab conflict. At the time I was surprised how well the book was received but I shouldn't have been. I was challenging the premise of theology in the language of theology. The book became a textbook in seminaries.

After writing *DFR* I tried to fill out the religious part by writing *TPR*. The book is clumsy and overwritten because I was trying to make sure that no one would confuse this with a book of Christian theology. I necessarily used many of the same words theology does but I was writing in a different language. Alas. The book was criticized for being bad theology.

My concern with "revelation" here is an educational one. The Christian Church(es) is now permanently fixed in a world of religious diversity. It can try to control the language and for a while it may have some success. But for its own health and for the well-being of the not-Christian majority, it needs linguistic bridges. For this purpose I find revelation to be an especially helpful word ("faith" is another though I think more restricted word). The Christian tradition has an invaluable contribution to make (the relation of knowing to death/resurrection, the person of Jesus in relation to the community of Judaism, transforming hope, etc.) but very simply and definitively: It doesn't own the word, it has no exclusive rights to control the defining.

The history of education in the United States has been strongly influenced by assumptions about "revelation." When Horace Mann was establishing the "public school" in Massachusetts he was fully conscious of the religious element. Mann speaks of "revealed religion" and "natural religion," probably unaware that that language was barely seventy-five years old. According to W. C. Smith, no one until the 18th century had said that it was *religion* that was revealed.[9] The 19th-century educator confidently assumed the distinction; he proposed that the common or natural religion be conveyed in the public school; the denominational religion was to be given in Sunday school. By what was more than a happy accident, the common religion turned out to be amazingly like a residual Christianity (one God, immortal soul, reward/punishment, etc.). Thus the 19th-century language for discussing religion in education was: The Catholics (Papists) on the right (denominational), the "Christians" in the center (common religion), and the Jews/atheists on the left (no religion).[10]

Because of an assumption about revelation (and a fear of a moral anarchy) the public school had always engaged in "religious education." Because of the peculiar split between a common religion and a denominational religion, the education has been rather poor from both directions. The Catholics were not so narrow or intolerant as earlier historians presumed. The "revisionist" historians of education now see the racial, class, and religious bias that has affected the school system. Unfortunately, the problem of the educational system is still with us today, including a failure to deal intelligently and fairly with religion. For everyone in the United States it is important that "religious education" be conceived so as to cut across the divisions that are damaging to our religious and educational lives.

The Model: School

Finally let me try to do just that, namely, conceptualize my (advocated) meaning of religious education. An advocative meaning, I've said, has to find some basis in what now exists. But instead of accepting "what exists" as equivalent to one setting and one moment, the advocator looks for something more both in the past (still with us, in us, and under us) and in other people beyond our village. The model of religious education is necessarily complex: two settings and several orientations within each setting. The two settings I call "school" and "laboratory" (a word I'm not entirely happy with but one connoting work, joint activity, and experiments).

For explaining the distinction of educational settings I would like to refer to a book by John Westerhoff who writes clearly and has a good sense of education.[11] Westerhoff says that the problem with religious education is that it has been tied to a "school paradigm" instead of a "community of faith-enculturation paradigm." Whatever the details of that second paradigm, I think it is clear that Westerhoff is fighting a battle similar to that of many people interested in educational reform today. Education and school are not to be equated. That is true, but there are opposite directions in which people go from that thesis. One is to cultivate educational forms to complement school; the other is to attack school in the name of individual liberty. The latter position is represented by Ivan Illich (and I'm afraid increasingly by John Holt). The effect of this attack, if there is an effect at all, is to reinforce the hold of school on education. I wouldn't put Westerhoff in this camp but by trying to replace a school paradigm with one other, he might get caught up into the unrealism of the "de-schoolers."

Whereas Illich's proposals are (in my terms) anticommunal, Westerhoff is keenly interested in the communal. The problem is that one might get the impression that the academic, scholarly, and rational have been overemphasized. But it is the academic side that is one of the weakest elements in religious education —explicitly as practiced in churches and implicitly (in my advocative meaning) as practiced in the public school. If one had to choose between them, it seems to me obvious that the church has been more successful in providing community/enculturation than in providing schools for studying religion. I am not dismissing Westerhoff's important point; he rightfully says that the church(es) has something valuable to offer education and religious education. But what I would also want affirmed is that the church is badly in need of schooling—not the poorly constituted church school of the 19th century but real schools in which religion can be taught/studied (i.e., critically examined and intellectually understood).

Within the school setting the study of religion could be (and is) sponsored by ecclesiastical, private, and public institutions. However, there are 2 distinct religious orientations within this setting. One is a study of religion from within a specific tradition with a feel for its inner life (often called "theology" by the church[es]). The other approach is the study of religion from some distance, that is, with at least temporary suspension of the assumptions of the religious group. This approach is not best called "objective" (as if one could step outside to some point of neutrality) but intersubjective (the particular being studied in relation to other particulars). This latter approach alone would be inadequate and perhaps damaging to a religious life. But together with the first, it is an indispensable element of a religious education today.[12]

Religion, as I have pointed out, has been part of the U.S. public school but it has not been taught/studied there. Ironically, in relation to religion the public school has been more of a church than a school. No greater step has been taken in developing an adequate "religious education" than the Supreme Court's decisions of the 1960s on religion and public education. The Court on the one hand banned mindless or imposed religious practices and on the other hand encouraged the study of religion. The Court did its job but educationalists have tended to repeat the Court's phrases (like Justice Goldberg's misleading "teach about religion") instead of developing a language of religious education.

The literature on the subject is bogged down in a language that is either ecclesiastical or anti-ecclesiastical. The Christian Church(es) can and should get into this context but it doesn't legitimately own the words that pertain to religious instruction whether in church-related schools or publicly sponsored schools and universities.

The Model: Laboratory

Within the other setting, which I call the laboratory, church language can be very helpful. Within the laboratory I distinguish 3 main orientations to learning: the family/community, the work site, the "retreat." Each of these is important for education today and in each of them the religious question can organically emerge. There is a triangular relation among the 3; none should be burdened with more than it can do. In religious terms each of them includes prayer and each of them can be a way of social transformation toward a religious vision.

The laboratory is connected to the school because only a religious body that is structured by these elements will have the courage and the resources to engage in the inquiry of the school. A religious body (e.g., church) that is composed of families/communities engaged in effective work and stepping back at times in "retreat" will want to study about itself and others. The existence of the laboratory is also an affirmation of other kinds of competence besides the academic. People often have educational resources in themselves that they don't recognize.

The family is an extremely important element in religious education but it shouldn't be romanticized as it often is by church officials. The family is already overburdened. Before there is talk of returning religious education to the family, church officials should provide communal surroundings for families and for the majority of people who do not live in father-mother-children units. Here is where the somewhat misleading interest in "adult education" should be directed: toward people at whatever age they are in whatever set of social relationships they are. We need learning within families, learning between children and other adults, learning between the very old and the very young, learning between families and all of society's "outsiders" (the divorced, widowed, homosexual, "retarded," etc.).

If the liturgy of the church(es) were really a family/community affair (and related to work, i.e., social action), then one could believe the high rhetoric of church documents on liturgy and education. I think that vast numbers in the Catholic Church have become disillusioned with the educational possibilities of the liturgy. But I think that one cannot simply give up on this point. For the sake of an adequate religious education we have to keep working at the linguistic and institutional form of church so that liturgy can blossom and give all of education a sacramental character.

My use of the word retreat here may seem out of place. But a funny thing happened to retreats as they (nearly) disappeared from the church(es). They got discovered by educationalists and psychologists.[13] (My meaning may therefore be closer to an older meaning of retreat than the more recent meaning in both Catholic and Protestant churches). Never has there been such a need for retreats in society, that is, a need to step back somewhere and be quiet within oneself. The contemplative element, which is appropriate to the retreat and complementary to liturgy, cannot be directly taught; nonetheless it is at the center of all education.

Retreat centers are especially needed in the middle of our cities. Great numbers of Catholics live there and, more important, so do millions of the dispossessed and suffering poor. These people need competent tools to improve their lot. The church(es) can do a little to respond to that need. But the problem is so overwhelming that the church(es) even at its best hardly makes a dent. What the church and church people can do well is to provide a place for a religious sense in the middle of the struggle. That's still not much and we church people ought to keep our claims modest. Nevertheless, I think it is a test of whether we are engaging in religious education at all.

There is a related point here that I would like to note. The Catholic language of catechist is one I can no longer identify with. I describe myself as a teacher, a word that I claim is wider than catechist. From the other side, church people say that catechist is wider than teacher. Actually both statements are true but in different senses. Teacher is wider than catechist in reference to institutions; teacher has currency outside the church whereas catechist doesn't. On the other hand, catechist can be wider than teacher with reference to activities engaged in. Teacher is largely controlled by the school form; catechist might include work with the laboratory form as well as school.

There is a crucial methodological issue here about ecclesiastical language. I and millions of other people remain suspicious. Catechist may be wider than teacher but catechesis remains one element within a religious education. A minister might do more things than a teacher but ministry does not embrace education. People in graduate programs these days say: "I'm interested in something bigger than religious education; I'm in pastoral ministry." I know what they are saying but I suggest they reconsider their giving up on education so easily. The operative meaning of "religious education" may be narrow but the term may be worth fighting for. If one wants to open up the Church to new possibilities one should recognize that words like "pastoral" or "ministry" are rather well controlled from within that church. I return to the point made in reference to Westerhoff: Before the church can claim to get beyond education—especially that of the school—it has to be sure that it can get so far.

The model I have presented leaves many points open for debate (e.g., the extent to which teachers can/should modify the behavior of students, how to plan/execute a course, how to run a graduate program of religious education). I am willing to discuss any such points once we're agreed that we're talking about education. Within education, religious spreads out in strange ways that, say, mathematical doesn't. From the start, religious challenges education rather than neatly finding its own little corner. Education needs the religious lest it close in on itself; religion needs a context of education so that the Christian church(es) does a respectable job of preserving within itself some of the elements of a religious education. But in the United States of the last quarter of the 20th century we are overdue in developing a meaning of "religious education" in which the church(es) and all interested parties can begin to participate.

Notes

1. W. Cantwell Smith, *The Meaning and End of Religion* (New York: Mentor, 1964).

2. Cf. Winthrop Hudson, *Religion in America*, 2nd ed. (New York: Scribner, 1973), pp. 300f.

3. Cf. Jürgen Habermas, *Knowledge and Human Interests* (Boston: Beacon, 1971); William Lee Miller, *Of Thee, Nevertheless, I Sing* (New York: Harcourt, 1975).

4. Cf. P. B. Medewan, "Are IQs Nonsense?" *New York Review of Books*, February 3, 1977, pp. 13ff.

5. John Westerhoff, *Will Our Children Have Faith?* (New York: Seabury, 1976).

6. New York: Abingdon, 1976.

7. My books are referred to in the text by initials. The cited books are:

   Theology of Revelation (TOR), 1966
   Experiences in Community (EIC), 1968
   Design for Religion (DFR), 1970
   The Present Revelation (TPR), 1972
   Religious Body (RB), 1974

8. Cambridge: Harvard Univ. Press, 1972

9. Smith, *The Meaning and End of Religion*, p. 41; on Horace Mann, cf. Michael Katz, *Class, Bureaucracy and School* (New York: Praeger, 1971), p. 37.

10. Cf. Josiah Strong, *Our Country*, ed. Jürgen Herbst (Cambridge: Harvard Univ. Press, 1963 [1891]).

11. Westerhoff, *Will Our Children Have Faith?*

12. For further development of this point, cf. Gabriel Moran, "Two Languages of Religious Education," *Living Light* 14 (Spring 1977): 7-15.

13. Cf. E. Fuller Torrey, *The Death of Psychiatry* (New York: Penguin, 1975), pp. 164-174.

The Challenge Ahead of Us

FRANÇOISE DARCY-BÉRUBÉ

Introduction

The Boston College Symposium Committee had asked four of the five panelists to present position papers on the Foundations of Religious Education. This was obviously a very broad topic and as it turned out each of the panelists understood it in a very different way. The consequences of this situation were both positive and negative. The positive one was the richness, importance, and variety of the problems that were brought up. The negative one was the practical difficulty of discussing in depth any of those problems. We were, if I might say, "all over the place!" And the final consequence was that the critical reactor, as Gabriel Moran put it, "was faced with an impossible task." This statement holds true not only for the two-day symposium but also for this critical essay. However this impossible task was and is both enriching and enjoyable and I decided to face it in the following way. Using both the papers and the recordings of the conversations I will try to present a critical reaction to some of the most important ideas and positions proposed or discussed by each panelist. In doing so I will have the opportunity to present some of my own ideas and positions with regard to some of the real foundational problems we have to face in religious education today in North America. In a brief conclusion I will express my fears, hopes, and wishes for the future.

Critical Reaction to the Position Papers

To anyone reflectively reading the four position papers it will appear obvious that in the format of a brief essay I can by no means deal with all the problems involved in each one. I will

111

choose to react only to those aspects of the author's thought that seem to me more relevant to my own preoccupations concerning the present situation of religious education.

To avoid getting involved at the start in dispute over the terms we should or should not use, I will speak about religious education in the broad sense it was intended in the symposium program. I will also speak all along from within the Roman Catholic tradition.

James Michael Lee: Some Key Issues in the Development of a Workable Basis for Religious Instruction

1. Introductory Remarks

Dr. Lee has made and still can make a significant contribution to religious education in this country. But I think it is honest to say that many educators react to his work with a certain defensiveness. This was apparent on our panel and in the audience at the symposium. It was my own initial reaction in reading his paper.

Trying to figure out the reasons for this attitude, I find two that seem to stand out. One is the behaviorist vocabulary of which many religious educators are suspicious. They are not accustomed to it, they do not understand it fully, and therefore many feel vaguely threatened by it. The second reason, it seems to me, could come from the style or manner in which Jim sometimes presents his ideas. He speaks of his work as "an overarching theoretical approach to religious instruction . . ." that "seeks to deal with all the phenomena falling under the entire spectrum of religious instruction" and is "the first attempt ever made to construct a comprehensive, systematic, integrated macrotheory of religious instruction." When he speaks or writes in these terms, many educators feel ill at ease with regard to this grandiose theory and apparently imperialistic project that does not even seem to leave room for discussion. They are afraid to be imprisoned in some kind of overstructured guidelines that, under the name of social science, would be just as rigid and constricting as the old-time approach of theological indoctrination. Because such statements stand out and capture the attention one does not notice sufficiently that some other statements seem to attenuate the first ones and that, if analyzed in detail, there are more nuances in Jim's thought than is apparent.

2. *The Positive Contribution of James M. Lee*

(a) *He rightly reacts against amateurism in religious education.* One of the great contributions of Dr. Lee is his strong reaction against "amateurism" in religious education or what he also calls "activists" who "by and large believe that the improvement of religion teaching comes about by 'tips,' gimmicks, or 'Mr. Fix-it' techniques rather than by practice that is everywhere rooted in and informed by theory."[1] Here I agree with Jim a hundred percent. And if he could really be heard on this, he would have rendered us a tremendous service. I do believe with Jim that the theory behind our educational activity must be brought into the open, critiqued, and clearly conceptualized. And it is interesting to realize that even very competent educators who may have excellent general educational perspectives and strategies can be caught in the act of not having sufficiently reflected on the theoretical basis of certain of their activities. Let me just give an example of what I mean by reporting a fragment of conversation from the symposium between Jim Lee and Tom Groome, knowing that Tom will not mind if I tease him a little about that.

In his discussion with Tom Groome, Jim rightly pointed out that we inevitably, if not knowingly, operate out of a theory. That is, we use empirical observation to prepare what we want to do and evaluate it. But oftentimes these theoretical assumptions are implicit, vague, and therefore not very effective. Sometimes they can be detrimental to our very goals, but, because they have not been explicated, they cannot be critiqued.

Tom, describing strategies he used with children, happened to say, "It worked well." Jim of course asked him, "Why do you say this? How can you say it?" Tom replied, "Well, they enjoyed it!" If we pushed that reaction further we could say: For Tom's teaching theory the criterion of success and effectiveness is that the children enjoy what they are doing!

Now even if this is partly true it is by no means a sufficient criterion and I am sure that Tom, precisely confronted with this statement, would agree with me. I remember a class of first graders who were absolutely fascinated for a full half-hour by a substitute teacher who told them, one after another, some of the most spectacular miracle stories of the Old and New Testaments. She was a marvelous narrator and the children enjoyed it tremendously. But how it helped the deepening and purification of their sense of God is another question! So I would fully support Jim's request for a more professional approach to the theoretical basis of religious instruction. One of the important questions he could help us solve here is what kind of taxonomy is fitted for religious instruction.

(b) *He focuses our attention on the religious instruction act.* Another of Jim's important contributions is that he clearly underlines the importance of the *religious instruction act*. As I will say later on, I do not totally share his understanding of that act, but I do feel he is right in bringing our attention to the instructional act. "Religious *instruction* [I underline instruction] *is* the religious instruction act." Within this act "theory and practice dynamically interact and should always flow out of and into this instructional act."

These statements should be clearly understood by all those who engage in program or curriculum design and this has not always been the case. In the two components that Jim distinguishes in the instructional act, "namely structural content and substantive content," the former has often been neglected and programs or curriculums designed mainly around substantive content. But it also happened the other way around. Whenever the dynamic interaction between the structural and substantive dimensions of the content of the act is inexistent, the religious instruction act itself is vitiated, deformed, and cannot be authentically fruitful.

(c) *He helps us understand better the importance of the interaction between the different variables in the teaching-learning situation.* Jim rightly asks us to study very carefully the interaction between the different variables in the teaching/learning situation, namely the teacher, the learner, the environment, and the subject content. If we took him seriously enough we would then understand how vitally important it is for us to get to know each of the individuals we are trying to teach. That means trying to know a child, for instance, not only in what he reveals of himself in the classroom, but in what kind of milieu of family he comes from, what are his or her particular temperament, personality traits, problems, dreams, and so forth.

I am not sure this would make our task easier, but I am sure it would make it much more fruitful. And furthermore I hope it would lead us to understand that certain settings and situations are in themselves obstacles to real education.

(d) *He underlines the necessity for graduate programs to give a much greater importance to the reflection on the theoretical basis of religious instruction.* I do agree that many graduate programs do not give enough importance to fundamental pedagogical perspectives and reflection. They rarely reach the balance between reflection on vision and tactics and too often are satisfied with presenting a display of materials with their "directions for use." This is perhaps one of the reasons why the criteria teachers use for choosing programs, audiovisuals, or other materials are so inadequate. One just has to stand for a few minutes at a publisher's booth at a congress and listen to the commentaries of the teachers choosing the books to understand what I mean!

These are a few aspects of Jim's contribution that can be of great help to us if we can listen to him with open minds, trying to really understand what he is saying and not letting ourselves be turned off by the behaviorist vocabulary he uses. Only once we have done that can we proceed to take a close, critical look at some of the shortcomings and dangers his theory implies.

3. Critiques and Questions about Some of James M. Lee's Ideas

(a) *He does not seem to see clearly the difference between faith and religious behavior.* This misunderstanding is crucial to the main critiques I will address to Jim's paper and to his reactions during the symposium. On page 2 of his paper Jim gives a very interesting definition of religion:

> Religion is that form of life-style which expresses and enfleshes the *lived relationship* a person enjoys with God as a conse-

quence of the *actualized fusion* in his self-system of that knowledge, belief, feeling, experience, and practice that in one way or another are connected with that which the individual or society perceives to be divine. (italics mine)

Let me note first of all that (unless I have been inattentive) this is the only time the expression "lived relationship" is used throughout the paper. This, to my mind, is very significant and points out sharply the fundamental problem I and many others have with Jim's theorizing. Everything Jim says in his paper can apply more or less to the different and separate elements of religion he enumerates in the second part of his definition: knowledge, belief, feeling, experience, and practice. To a certain extent Jim's central preoccupation to be able to "explain, predict, and verify behavioral outcomes" can eventually apply to each of these realities.

But by no means can it apply to what he rightly calls the "actualized fusion of these elements in the lived relationship with God." Let me explain this further. This lived relationship with God is what traditional Catholic theology calls faith, hope, and charity, or what Paul describes as life in the Spirit. And this is primarily a gift from God, whose influence is interior to our own spirit:[2]

The Spirit himself bears witness to our spirit that we are sons of God (Rom. 8:16).

No one can say Jesus is the Lord if the Spirit is not with him (I Cor. 12:3).

God's love has been poured into our hearts through the Holy Spirit which has been given to us (Rom. 5:5).

If we live by the Spirit, let us also walk by the Spirit (Gal. 5:25).

If this holds true, then there are two fundamental variables that Jim overlooks in his theorizing, namely God's free gift and action of revealing himself and taking the initiative to offer his love and call us to faith on the one hand, and man's freedom to accept or reject this gift and this call on the other. The most sophisticated instructional theory and practice cannot give or increase faith, hope, and charity; they cannot explain, predict, or measure the evolution of that "lived relationship with God" that Lee calls religion.

Because of this fundamental and crucial distinction that Jim does not make, I cannot accept his statement that his theory is an "*overarching comprehensive,* systematic integrated macrotheory of religious instruction," which is seeking to "deal with *all* the phenomena falling under the *entire spectrum* of religious instruction" (italics mine). Therefore, in my opinion, his theory is not, in the sense he thinks it is, a real foundational theory. It is only a foundational teaching theory for certain limited aspects of religion that in his own words "can be taught," like knowledge, attitudes, practices, and so forth. But his theory is not foundational nor operational vis-à-vis the global phenomena of "the lived relationship with God" that an individual chooses to engage in by answering God's call.

This is not to say that his theory cannot be very useful to improve the way we teach doctrine or church history, for instance, or propose prayer experiences, or try to induce progress in moral judgment and behavior in the light of the Gospel. But we must be aware that by doing all this and doing it the best we can with the help of a good theory, we are only "preparing the way for the Lord," we are only bringing people to the threshold of an awakening or a deepening of their own lived relationship with God. As Berard Marthaler said during the symposium as a critique addressed to Jim: "He has taken an instructional model that is a part and parcel of the enterprise of education and of religious education. And what he has done with this single model is to erect a theory, and then he has come back with that theory and has tried to co-opt everything else and force it into that package." This central problem is probably the source of the two other difficulties I see in Jim's theory and ideas.

(b) *He does not fully understand the necessary relationship between theology and religious instruction.* Everybody agrees nowadays that theological instruction and religious instruction are not the same. Although many problems have arisen around the nature of theology today, as Gabriel Moran pointed out, I will use the word here as "a critical reflection on the Tradition of the Church," and, particularly for the following paragraphs, in reference to the *Corpus Doctrinae.*

All pedagogy, because it aims, as Jim writes, "to help a being actualize what it is meant to be," defines itself more or less explicitly in reference to a certain image of man, and when it is used in religious instruction, in reference to an image of God also. Jim rightly points out that the pedagogical practice must be informed and shaped by an instructional theory that is explicitly conceptualized so that it can be analyzed, critiqued, and improved. In the same way I would insist on the importance of bringing into light and clearly expressing the underlying theology that inspires and shapes both the behavioral outcomes the theory strives to facilitate and, indirectly, the pedagogical means or strategies it proposes.

It would be very important for Jim to spell out clearly the vision of man, of God, of Church, and of Christian life that inspires his theory. In the discussion he seemed very reluctant to do that and fell back on the "doctrine" of the Church. But the doctrine of the Church is an abstraction; it only exists as theologically interpreted.

Jim is not a theologian and we do not ask him to be one. But we do ask him to state explicitly the theology he has implicitly interwoven in his instructional theory. This, I believe, would allow for a much more fruitful dialogue with him. Coming back to the instructional act he so accurately describes, I would like to point out to Jim that theology, in my opinion, does have something to do not only with the substantive content, as he somewhat reluctantly acknowledges, but also with the structural content. It is perfectly true that "there are no teaching techniques that are distinctively Christian." But there are teaching techniques that can be opposed to a Christian vision of man, of God, and of their mutual relationship in faith and love. For example certain teaching techniques used by the Moonies, or even by Billy Graham in his crusades are, for me, unacceptable from a theological standpoint because they are manipulative. I am not implying here that Jim suggests such techniques but I am saying that theology does have something to say even about teaching techniques and/or structural content, and cannot accept them without discernment.

(c) *There is some ambiguity in Jim's statements about religion as a life-style.* Reacting, I believe, against the cognitive approach he thinks is proposed by Tom Groome, Jim affirmed many times that he is aiming at a life-style and I agree with him of course that religion can be said to be a life-style. But that word can hide many ambiguities. The Jehovah's Witnesses insist also on the life-style and I recently saw on television a remarkable film on how the militant cells of Maoists are aiming at and succeeding in modifying the life-style of local populations in different country towns of China.

Modification of a life-style can be the result of efficient brainwashing, indoctrination, pressure, manipulation. This can be done in violent authoritarian ways, but it can also be done in very subtle ways.

The transformation of the life-style that Christian Tradition calls conversion and continuing growth in faith and love flows from the spiritual experience of a "lived relationship with God," that is to say, from the mystical dimension of religion. This means that it is out of the reach of any pedagogical technique. It cannot be the result of conditioning by manipulating variables.

Once again I am not saying that instruction cannot do anything in this respect. It can and should do a lot but it must be aware of its own limits and perhaps the expressions "behavior modifications" or "behavioral outcomes" should be nuanced (and commented on) so that it is clear that they do not replace the "change of heart," openness to the Spirit, and free self-giving that is the real challenge of religious education.

After reading all this I am sure that Jim will be tempted (but he is too kind to do it) to label me as an advocate of the "blow theory." But I don't think I am in the way he means it! Indeed I am a deep believer in the constant creative action of the Spirit in all human lives but by no means do I think that this faith in the Spirit dispenses us from the kind of very hard and scientific work Jim has done and which we should learn from him to do on the technical aspects of the instructional act.

Conclusion

In conclusion I would like to make the following statements. Probably because Dr. Lee's ideas have often been misunderstood or misinterpreted, he sometimes seems too defensive and unwilling to accept real questioning and discussion of his ideas. And because of his very strong social science formation and orientation he seems to have some difficulty in grasping accurately the precise point people are trying to make when they are addressing him in a language different from his, that is, philosophical, poetic, theological, or artistic. For those two reasons and perhaps others I ignore, Jim often seems to elude the precise questions we ask him or to displace them, which makes real dialogue very difficult. I deeply regret this because I do feel that Jim, because of his competence as well as his personal qualities and deep Christian commitment, has a great deal to bring to certain aspects of religious instruction today.

I do hope I am not being unfair to Jim in saying this but I feel that if he cannot accept the limits of his theory and enter an open critical dialogue, then his ideas can be dangerous because they can lead educators to think that their task is mainly a matter of technical competence in organizing variables. If this happens then the most religious educators can achieve is ideological conversion and enrollment instead of leading persons to the threshold of the endless and unpredictable adventure of a lived relationship with God, which for me is faith.

Tom Groome: Christian Education for Freedom:
A "Shared-Praxis Approach"

1. Introductory Remarks

It was indeed stimulating to listen to Tom Groome defend his ideas or attack those of others with his Irish passion and impetuosity! He is just out of many years of study and intensive reading, working on his doctoral thesis; this was apparent in the fifty-nine footnotes he added to his paper, which I read with great interest.

My general impression in reading Tom and listening to him is that he has put together in his own original way many trends of thought and of action that have been emerging in the past decades and have been influencing his own educational work and that of many others. In conceptualizing these trends and proposing the personal approach he describes as "shared praxis," he renders us a great service because he helps us see both its great importance and fruitfulness and also its limits. I will try to elaborate somewhat on both aspects. In doing so I will not follow the same outline as I did to analyze Jim Lee's paper; I will simply discuss one after the other the two parts of Tom's paper, expressing as they come my points of agreement and disagreement, and the questions I would like to see Tom further analyze, deepen, or expand.

2. *Discussion of Part One: In Quest of a Language and Purpose*

I do not wish to discuss here completely the overall language question because I prefer to take it up at the end of my paper after having reacted to the four symposium papers. However, I do wish to discuss Tom's proposition about calling our common task "*Christian* Education for *Freedom*" (italics mine) because this proposition has a direct bearing on the approach itself. I do not agree with either italicized term for the following reasons.

"Christian education," I must say, was appealing to me till the symposium. I often used it myself instead of "religious education." But, after reading Jim Lee's criticisms of it and hearing Gabe explain the negative and misleading overtones of that expression in broad circles of population in the United States, I accept these criticisms and wonder if the expression can be reclaimed as Tom thinks it can. If it could I would be happy to use it.

Tom writes that he wants a term more specific than "religious" to qualify "education" and that if we are working in a specific tradition, that tradition should be named. Why then not be really specific in naming that tradition, as Jim Lee suggests, and talk about *Catholic* education? I am not saying that I advocate this, but I am underlying the fact that there are many different traditions under the term Christian and that if one wants to be specific, perhaps the term "Christian" is misleading.

I would also like to argue with Tom on the meaning of the word "education." In the paragraph about education we find two definitions and it is not clear if the second is a commentary on the first or a different definition. Tom writes: "By education I mean the deliberate and intentional attending in the present to the future possibility of the total person and the community." I can accept that definition, even if I don't necessarily think it is the best or only one. But he writes immediately after: "Education is a concerted attempt by people called educators to enable others with themselves *to confront* the limit situations of life and push beyond them" (italics mine).

In this second statement I feel that the description of education is too directly and exclusively related to limit situations. I wonder if the idea of fullness of life, of humaneness, would not be more comprehensive and more faithful to the scope of the first definition relating education to the future possibility of the total person. As educators, are we not concerned with helping people become fully human, that is to say capable and free to wonder, to discover, to love, to create, to shape their lives, and as part of this humaneness, to search for meaning and happiness, to confront limit situations, and to reach for the transcendent? This is why I find the second part of Tom's description of education too restrictive and implicitly too oriented by his axiological choice for freedom as the purpose of religious education.

As for the expression "for freedom," which is supposed to describe the *overall purpose* of Christian education, I cannot agree with it either.

I am completely in agreement with Tom when he writes that "it is the task of the Christian people in all ages to constantly and critically reclaim their faith tradition in the light of contemporary consciousness." I also agree with Hodgson that this perspective of freedom can provide "a hermeneutical framework for interpreting the biblical and theological tradition afresh." But in my opinion this does not justify setting up freedom as the overall purpose of religious education.

Freedom, for me, is not the overall aim or goal of religious education; it is a means, a path to, a condition of fullness of life. Indeed Jesus came to free man individually and collectively, and Tom has very beautiful pages on the subject. But, as Jesus himself said, "I came so that you may have life and life in abundance" (Jn. 10:10; 17:2). Indeed religious education and education in general should strive to free people from everything that hinders from within (internal forces) or from without (social, economic, political forces) the full development of their life, of their humaneness. Born to be free, yes, but free to become what you are called to be, a human being, a son or daughter of God; free to live to the full by sharing in God's own life, in his creative love. I believe that the idea of fullness of life is much more comprehensive than the one of freedom, even if freedom is at the heart of our faith. The idea of freedom is extremely congenial to the critical consciousness of our time and rightly so. It is one of the basic biblical themes and will always be. It is very relevant to use this "hermeneutical framework for interpreting the biblical and theological tradition afresh" in designing curricula, educational experiences, and so forth. But to designate freedom as the overall purpose of religious education (and writing it in its very name) is a different thing. I believe it is too partial (as opposed to evoking the overall purpose) and too linked to a contemporary consciousness that by definition is subject to constant change. Though I do not agree with the term then, I am not proposing anything yet to replace it.

Before coming to the central part of Tom's paper on shared praxis with which I feel in deep accord, let me underline a last point of disagreement.

In his description of the three dimensions of freedom, which contains very accurate and pertinent statements, I wonder if Tom has not been a little simplistic. Basically of course I agree with his description of these dimensions and with the fact that they are interrelated and that we must work to make the three possible. But I do feel that he is too affirmative and categorical in certain of his judgments.

When he makes his own Hodgson's statement that there cannot be "an inner freedom in the context of an outer bondage and an alien world," I disagree. I think there are innumerable examples of people who in extremely difficult situations where they were indeed fiercely oppressed, living under totally inhuman conditions, did in fact manifest an incredible spiritual freedom. To mention only one example let me name Solzhenitsyn. But how many in the Nazi Germany of the forties and today in the jails of Brazil or Russia or Chile manifest that spiritual freedom can eventually exist without social freedom? Once again this is not to say that we must not work for social freedom and that for the great majority it is probably a necessary condition for spiritual freedom, but my point is that Tom's assertion here seems to me too categorical.

As for psychological freedom's being a precondition for spiritual freedom, here again I agree of course theoretically. However I think the problem is much more complex than Tom seems to think. First because psychological freedom is always relative and secondly because this question of the relationship between psychological health, integrity, and freedom, and spiritual life has been studied for many years and the researchers are far from having reached any definitive conclusion. As a matter of fact many of those we call "mystics" did not seem to enjoy totally this psychological freedom Tom assigns as a precondition for spiritual freedom!

What I want to say here is that the world of perfect psychological, social, and spiritual freedom Tom describes in a brief page is an unreal, imaginary world. I believe that it is in this real world, where psychological and social freedom are always relative and precarious, that we must work with the creative energy of the Spirit to grow toward freedom. Even more than being "condemned to freedom" as Sartre says (quoted by Tom), I believe we are "called to freedom" (Gal. 5:1). And perhaps it is paradoxical but not untrue that in a sense the initial gift of freedom that the risen Christ brings us through his Spirit is one of the forces that sets us moving to desire and struggle for psychological and social freedom.

3. Discussion of Part 2: An Approach of Shared Praxis

In my opinion the second part of Tom's paper is the most original and valuable. Certain pages are indeed of excellent quality and could be a significant contribution to the present reflection on religious education. I will first react to the general presentation of the approach, then I will come back to specific aspects of it.

(a) *The two major contributions of the Shared-Praxis approach:*

● *The introduction of a critical dimension in religious education:* As Tom points out, the word "praxis" is one of the "in" terms! In French-speaking Canada it has even given birth to the word "praxeology," which dominates right now the pastoral reflection at the University of Montreal.

Tom summarizes well, although briefly, this trend of thought. The major contribution of the shared-praxis approach is that it brings into the basic perspective and into the process of religious education a *critical dimension* that is badly needed and that is for me of vital importance to the life of the Church. When dealing with the socialization model I will comment on this in greater detail.

● *The conceptual and operational framework of shared praxis:* The second contribution I wish to underline is the way Tom clearly points out the danger of positing what he calls "the Story and the Vision as fetishized ideologies that themselves control our present."

He summarizes very accurately this fundamental and original insight when he writes: "Thus, the present, while it is critiqued by the Story and Vision, must also be posed as a critique of the past Story as we know it and as a critique of our present notion of the Vision to whose building we are to contribute" (pp. 17-18). This principle of "present dialectical hermeneutics," as he calls it, is at the heart of his method and Tom is the first one, to my knowledge, to have presented it so clearly and made it operational in his strategy.

As Tom said himself during the symposium, many people including himself have been working intuitively along those lines in the past decade, but he renders us a great service in decomposing and analyzing for us in a conceptual framework the basic dialectical rhythm of the method. He also pushes it forward and enriches it significantly in showing how the present can and should also be a critique of the Story and the Vision.

The five steps Tom proposes to operationalize his basic perspectives are well articulated and coherent; it is a pity, though, that he did not elaborate on them in greater detail and present them in a more concrete way in his paper, because some concepts, such as present action, life situation, experience, future action, remain imprecise.

As for the language Tom uses and the justification he gives of it, I will come back to that later. What I would like to do now after having emphasized the very significant value of the shared-praxis approach is to draw attention to its limits. I will deal both with the basic perspective and with the strategy.

(b) *The limits of the shared-praxis approach:*

● *A limit in the vision of religious education:* As I said in the preceding pages, the significant contribution of Tom's approach is that it brings into the basic perspective and process of religious education a very important dimension, which is the *critical dimension*. But the *very contribution* of the approach sets *also its limit* because it is only one of the dimensions of religious education, at least as I understand it. And this brings us back to the basic disagreement I had with Tom in my discussion of the first part of his paper, namely the disagreement about assigning freedom as the overall purpose of religious education.

Indeed he is consistent with himself and his axiological choice of freedom, but he is also inevitably, and without joking, limited if not imprisoned by it. Because he is so axiologically oriented toward freedom as the goal of religious education he is too unilaterally sensitive to the critical dimension of it. Yet there are other dimensions to religious education as there are to Christian life. Let me just mention the lyrical or poetic dimension of the human-Christian life with its double aspect of wonder/contemplation and celebration. This dimension to me is as essential as the critical dimension and one needs another type of theory/method to awaken and develop that dimension.

There is also a lived active experience of Christian life that is part of religious education in my opinion. Some have called it the political dimension (this adjective being taken in its ancient and noble sense of service of the "polis," the city); others have called this the social dimension of Christian life. Anyway this brings us to the fact that the limitation of Tom's basic perspective has its bearing on his strategy.

His approach was criticized by at least two of the other panelists as being exclusively cognitive. I don't think I agree with that because the five-step strategy, if well mastered, involves very deeply the emotional life of the participants and orients them toward action. But my criticism would be that it is —as presented in the paper—exclusively verbal. Therefore, paradoxically, Tom's approach is more intellectual than concretely "praxeological."

For Tom, in praxis, "the primary object of reflection is the *subject doing the reflecting*" (italics mine)[3] and the "social context" mediating that subject. But for me this reflection on the subject is only part of the dialectical process of praxis, which must include *real action*, or what we call more precisely *intervention* in the outside world. Reflection on the subject and the personal and social genesis of his/her ideas and attitudes is part of reflecting on the action but does not replace the acting.

In other terms, I feel that shared praxis should include, if it is to be as fruitful as it can be, not only shared reflection but *shared action*. The way Tom describes "present action" in his paper leads us to think that this action is always the action of reflecting together on a particular topic or issue. This is where I feel that perhaps Tom has not totally utilized one of the most powerful insights we can gain from both Marx and Paulo Freire. What really changes people, educates them, is not only reflecting on the "subject doing the reflecting," as Tom proposes, but entering concretely the dialectical process of action/reflection—in other terms, not only arousing "a critical consciousness" based on critical self-analysis, which can lead to action, but carrying out that action, which in turn arouses new questions, new insights, that will enrich the hermeneutical experience of interpretation that in turn will enrich, reorient, and so forth, the action. I am not saying that the group process of critical reflection on the "subject doing the reflecting" and the "social context that mediates it" is not good or effective. I am saying it is excellent but would be even more fruitful and complete if it did include that kind of action in which one directly confronts the outside world to carry out in it some concrete project.

This perspective of the formative power of action is present, I believe, in the two official documents on youth ministry and on adult catechumenate. But these documents fail to include the explicit critical dimension of shared praxis. This is where I feel the encounter of the two perspectives could be very rich.

● *Limits in the possibility of using the five-step strategy:* Here again the very nature of the theory-method (from which its power comes) also sets its limits of utilization. It is based on two elements: critical reflection and going back and forth from the present to past and future. Therefore it presupposes in the learners the capacity for critical thinking and a sense or awareness of historical time. For a developmental psychologist this immediately excludes young children from the reach of the method. This seemed obvious to all of the panelists (except Tom!) and most of the audience at the symposium. However, I would like to qualify this statement.

Concerning the historical time question first. A very interesting scientific study was published in Louvain a few years ago on the religious mediations in the child's world.[4] It studied in particular the eucharistic symbols. One of its findings brings out the fact that it is at around twelve years of age that the child becomes capable of integrating intellectually (and not only expressing verbally, which he can do sooner of course) the living symbolic relation between the Lord's Last Supper and the celebration of the Eucharist. This means that the real dialectical interaction between the present action and the past Story could only begin to be grasped around that time. This, I believe, holds true also for the future.

However, it is important to note here that if the historical sense of time is late to appear, the personal or existential sense of this time precedes it. This is why helping the child reflect critically on his own life experience in the very near past begins to be possible when he is around seven or eight years old. But this is something else than shared Christian praxis and it has been present in religious education procedures and materials for many years now.

(c) *Shared Praxis as a constant dimension of religious education and Christian life:*

Having pointed out why I feel shared praxis as such cannot be used with children under twelve years of age, I wish to underline the fact that, in my opinion, it should be a constant and normal dimension or aspect not only of religious education during adolescence and right into adulthood but that it is so to speak a normal dimension of Christian life. This should be the case for all those to whom Christian life means not only constant growing and maturing but also getting involved and taking their share of responsibility in any realm of activity: social, political, educational, or religious. I also think it is a condition of health for the pastoral ministry in the Church.

(d) *Practical problems involved in introducing educators to a shared-praxis approach in religious education:*

If one feels—and I do—that we should try to introduce educators to the shared-praxis approach, I think it is of great importance that we be well aware of the practical problems involved. I see two main categories of question to be faced:

- *structural changes:* because shared praxis can be effective only with small groups and should (this is wishful thinking on my part) if possible include common projects (real action to be part of the dialectical process);
- *teacher formation:* because to act as a facilitator in a shared-praxis group requires a profoundly different formation from the one presently given in most schools of education and/or religious education, and a very different approach to teaching from that which is current in the country.

The "epistemological shift" Tom mentions in his paper is a kind of conversion of mentality that has both a theological and an educational dimension. An important part of that teacher formation would be the development of a sense of discernment and a great respect for the individual person.

The kind of sharing required by shared praxis is very deep and very personal. Maybe everyone is not apt for that kind of sharing because of certain character traits. Or maybe no one is *always* ready for it because of certain experiences or emotional problems one can go through in the course of life. I am sure that Tom would be the first one to claim the necessity of respecting all these differences. But group pressure or implicit teacher pressure can be very powerful and finally very manipulative in subtle ways. When one feels in a group that everyone expects each to share and one really doesn't feel like doing it for one reason or another, it does create a tense situation for the one who feels forced to do it. The facilitator should be trained to discern and respect those difficulties.

I also think that however important the critical dimension may be to spiritual maturation, this tool should be handled with care so as to help people face the level and kind of questioning for which they are ready and which can help them and be a means of progress. If the critical reflection is too abrupt or too deep for their degree of readiness they will close up through fear instead of opening up to a broader vision of reality and a critical appropriation of their faith.

It is also probable that shared praxis will meet some resistance from large circles who will be afraid of the "subversive" dimension of such an approach. The method will have to be judged by the quality of the Christian life that will slowly manifest itself in the people and communities that will use it. Some will call those manifestations "behavioral outcomes," other "fruits of the Spirit." What is sure is that they will be as always the visible sign that the energy of the Spirit works from within man's own creative activity.

Conclusion

To conclude this analysis of Tom's promising work I would suggest that he use his critical reflection on his own theory-method so as to improve it and bring it to maturation.

To accomplish this Tom would benefit from open dialogue with the other panelists. For instance Tom could be enriched by discussion with Gabe both on his concept of revelation and on the importance of the contemplative element in religious education. I also believe that Tom could learn from Jim Lee the necessity to explicate more clearly the technical aspects of the teaching/ learning process of shared praxis, and the importance of clarity and precision in vocabulary. This does not mean that I wish Tom would take up a behavioral vocabulary! But I do think he has some work to do on language precision. As a matter of fact his paragraph on the language of shared praxis was quite weak. Moreover it would be very fruitful both for Tom and for Berard Marthaler to find out more precisely how the shared-praxis approach could and should be part of a socialization model, and how the critical dimension of education needs to be completed by the other ones in a global project of religious education.

Through this dialogue and critical reflection I hope Tom will be led to reconsider the place he assigns to freedom as the overall purpose of religious education (Christian education in his terms). Assigning freedom as the purpose of his theory/method, which is dealing with one of the dimensions of Christian life and education, namely the critical one, is fine. But assigning freedom as the overall purpose of religious (Christian) education as if it covered all its dimensions is, in my opinion, a mistake.

I also think that Tom will have to accept, just like Jim, the limits of his theory/method. If he does he will then resist the temptation of trying to overextend its reach. He will recognize that shared praxis cannot deal with all the dimensions of religious education and that it cannot be used with children. When theory or method are at stake I believe it is impossible that "one size fits all!"

Finally let me express once again my conviction that Tom, by bringing into religious education more explicitly than it ever was the critical dimension of Christian life, will make a very significant contribution to the quality of life in the Church.

Berard Marthaler: Socialization As a Model for Catechetics

1. Introductory Remarks

I was indeed impressed with Father Marthaler's very elaborate paper and happy to find out that we shared the common preoccupation of interdisciplinary work in the area of religious education, although he has probably been more influenced by sociology and I by psychology. Berard's purpose is both modest—he says he is only proposing one model among others possible—and at the same time ambitious, because he did try to be so comprehensive that he would cover all the ground. This is apparent for example in the way he included Jim Fowler's research in his paper.

I would like to say right away that I am in fundamental agreement with Berard's statement that "the socialization model is useful for explaining and interpreting many of the varied activities that are carried on in the name of religious education." However we are dealing here with a model that is not only proposed as a way of *explaining* and *interpreting* what happens in religious education; we are dealing here with a model for action, a model that is meant to inspire and shape a pedagogy. The model Berard proposes has an implicit "ought" to it. I am not criticizing this, it is a normal use of a model; but I am bringing it to light because this is where and why I feel it is important to bring in a critical analysis of the model.

I tend to think that in the years to come the socialization model will have a great influence on the course of events in religious education in the United States and Canada. This impact will have different causes. One is the intrinsic value and quality of Berard's work, a second is the great influence and power attached to Berard's positions, and the third is the fact that Berard has been very close to the team preparing the *National Catechetical Directory* and the socialization model's influence is pervasive throughout the *Directory*. Because of this probable—and desirable—impact of Berard's model I will try to carefully analyze its potentially dangerous implications and this will bring me to describe under what conditions we can overcome these dangers and use the model to the best advantage of the quality of religious education.

2. *Critical Analysis of the Socialization Model*

As I have just stated, I basically support the socialization model with the restrictions and conditions I will later describe. I will not detail here its advantages as Berard himself did that in his paper. However, I would like to comment on a statement Gabe made about it during the symposium. This will introduce my critical remarks.

Gabe stated that in his opinion "socialization was more a fact of life than a model." I think it is very true in the sense that whether we think of it or not we are being socialized. But this process, especially when it becomes "intentional socialization" as proposed here, is linked to an axiology, a vision of God, of man, and of Church. Furthermore, when it becomes an operative model it takes on the power associated with that transformation. This is why it is important to unveil, disclose, bring into the open, this underlying axiology.

Berard did an excellent job in summarizing through the first part of his paper the socialization process in general. I will not comment on this part but rather concentrate on parts II and III of his paper. Here again, however, I will have to limit myself to essentials because Berard touches too many aspects of reality and

I cannot think of discussing them all in the format of this essay. I will organize my reflections around three topics.

(a) *The socialization model tends to imprison religious education in a transmitting-maintaining process:*

Sociological research as well as everyday observation overwhelmingly proves the basic conservatism of societies. Any social group tends to educate its children in its own image and likeness. The whole power and weight of the socializing process tends to make it repetitive and self-perpetuating rather than creative. The stronger the educational structures in a society, the greater is the risk that the society will imprison itself in this "maintenance" attitude. The story of the Catholic Church is indeed an excellent illustration of that risk and if we listen to Ellis Nelson it is not the only one: "The problem of mainline Protestant Churches is that the process of transmitting a tradition is working too well—it is producing in the rising generation what the adults actually believe."[5]

I do not want to play a numbers' game and bring out in detail the number of times Berard uses a "maintenance"-oriented vocabulary; this is obvious to anyone reading the paper. But it is very significant—as was noted at the symposium—that only at the very end of his long essay did Berard mention the fact that the socialization process should imply a "transforming" aspect with regard to the culture and the community. Berard himself must have felt somewhat uneasy about this because he acknowledged not having emphasized this aspect. But I think it would be more accurate to say that he did not explicitly mention it before that and in no way explained how this transforming aspect could be included in the process. Just as I critiqued Tom for being too exclusively preoccupied with the emancipatory aspect of religious education, in the same way I critique Berard for being too exclusively oriented toward its maintenance aspect.

What I would like to make clear though in this debate is that the risk we are discussing—Berard being out of the picture—is inherent to the socialization model. This is why we need an explicit and effective antidote. I would like to propose shared praxis as the "positive antidote" that should be "built into" the very process of "intentional socialization." This would have two advantages. The first one is that intentional socialization would have an "alarm-system" and a "regulation-system" built into its very process, which would ensure that it is not becoming over-powering. The second is that it would also benefit from a built-in dynamic principle of constant renewal and progress. I believe that if shared praxis, based on Tom's principle of present dialectical hermeneutics, really became part of the intentional socialization process from adolescence up, this would have a far-reaching and even unpredictable revitalizing effect on the whole life of the Church: its liturgy, its theology, its structures, and mainly the quality of community life and witness. This in turn would benefit education itself if it is as we all think a "community affair."

Let me make this more concrete by commenting on one example concerning the document *A Vision of Youth Ministry,* which Berard mentions in his paper. In some of his best pages Berard describes catechesis as community education and after commenting on the bishops' document on youth he writes:

> The young are socialized through an interaction with the adult community which witnesses to faith and provides role models for the youth to imitate and emulate. They acquire a religious identity by taking as their own the creedal formulas, rites, the activities and other emblems that symbolize the corporate sol-idarity of the Catholic community.

I agree perfectly with Berard and with the document when they state the importance of that interaction between the adult community and the adolescents. But I would like to stress the importance for the community of adult preparation, utilizing a shared-praxis approach. This, I believe, would perhaps avoid the so frequent repetition of the following pattern: A closely knit group of young adolescents at the "conventional ideological" stage three of Fowler's[6] developmental schema is very actively involved under the influence of some dedicated and enthusiastic adults; all youth activities are booming, the future seems promis-ing. But after five or six years what do we see? Often the young, who are now in their late teens or early twenties, have taken three main directions depending on their types of personality. Some have neatly fitted into the daily routine of parish life without going through any crisis. They smoothly passed from enrollment in the youth group to enrollment in usual parish activities. They don't have many questions and if they do have one they usually go to a church authority to find the answer. Unless some rather trauma-tic event later breaks into their lives and shakes up their inner security, they will probably remain all along at stage three of "synthetic-conventional faith" and will raise their children with that attitude and spirit.

Other members of the youth group are still with it as young leaders. They were probably among the most gifted for social interaction. They are enthusiastic, generous, responsible. They remain very close to the adult leaders who keep them busy and involved. They are very effective with the young teens. Perhaps they went through brief moments of questioning and crisis, but the support from the group and the adult leaders was so strong and they were so involved that they couldn't delve too deeply into these difficulties, and seemed to overcome them rapidly. These youngsters often take on a leadership role in the adult community and this is the only thing that differentiates them from the preced-ing group, because both remain in reality at the same synthetic-conventional stage. Here again the "transmitting-maintaining sys-tem" will work well under their leadership in the parish. However experience shows that among the youngsters who followed this pattern, some during adulthood go through the stage-four crisis they avoided during their adolescence. Everyone knows that adolescence crises, when they are lived by an adult, are often very traumatic and destructive because they come too late; the personality is no longer adapted to them, it does not have the plasticity nor the youthful vitality it had, the life pattern is struc-tured and the future not open as it was during adolescence; these crises often end up in bitterness, despair, apathy, or revolt. As an adult man facing this situation told me one day: "They did not let me really live through the questions and crises of my adoles-cence, they tried to protect me from it by keeping me so involved. And now, I have made a mess of my life and I don't really know what my faith means to me!"

A third subgroup of that initial youth group could be called the dropouts. There are many kinds of "church dropouts" and varied reasons given for dropping out. Here I just want to analyze the case of those we could call "critics." Because of a critical mind or a very strong urge toward personal freedom and authenticity they gradually felt ill at ease in the very well organized, structured, and controlled activities and closed-circuit mentality of the youth group and of the parish. They didn't feel there was real room for open questions and critiques in the Church, they were not content with the "role models" presented to them to "imitate and emulate": They wanted to create! So they went their own way to be able to become really themselves, to learn the real taste of freedom and responsibility at their own risk. And they rejected what they called "the system." As one of them told me one day: "I didn't think I could stay in the Church and really be free and creative. In the Church everything is settled!" Often those young adults dedicate themselves to social or political causes and remain at a distance from the Church.

Of course this picture is, to an extent, a caricature; many adults have matured one way or the other in the Church! However, I do think my description has a lot of truth to it. Now my contention is that if the adult community socializing these adolescents had been prepared and educated itself in the line of shared praxis the situation I described would have been much different. Because they would have been interacting with adults for whom questioning and critical reflecting were part of the Christian way of life, part of work in the Church, the "critics" would have felt much more at home in the Church. They would have realized that they were not so much part of a system, or "caught up" in it as they say, as part of a pilgrim community, always on its way, changing, responding to the call of the Spirit by interpreting the signs of the time and imaginatively creating the future. Their critical and free minds would have been a means of growth for themselves and the community.

As for those who never grew up because they were unconsciously afraid of the uncertainty that could come out of critical questioning, they would have been helped to face this necessary phase of destruction and they would have learned that faith is not a comfortable "having-all-the-answers" but rather that "questioning is the piety of thought" as Heiddeger so beautifully wrote.

And the young leaders who were kept so busy that they did not have the leisure or the encouragement to go to the depth of their moments of questioning and therefore mature—those, while still developing their leadership capacities, would have integrated the critical dimension of Christian life. This would have allowed them to mature and considerably enriched the quality of their own Christian life and that of their leadership.

To sum up this long development I believe that without a shared-praxis dimension the socialization model can imprison religious education in its transmitting-maintaining aspect. But with that critical dimension it can, while ensuring the maintenance aspect, go beyond it and favor the transforming and liberating aspects too.

- *The socialization model runs the risk of fostering ideological internalization rather than faith.*

In the first part of his paper Berard, using Berger and Luckmann accurately, describes the dialectical process of socialization in its three "major moments": externalization, objectification, and internalization. Internalization, he writes, is "the term used to describe the reassimilation into consciousness of the objectified world of meanings."

In the second part of the paper Berard attempts to clarify somewhat the very complex problem of the relationships between faith and beliefs. Faith is seen as "a basic orientation, a fundamental attitude," described by David Tracy as "primal and often non-conceptual"; and, says Berard, "specific beliefs mediate its meaning." With Westerhoff, Richard McBrien, and others, Berard seems to agree that "faith cannot be taught." Therefore he concludes: "To be socialized in a particular religion is more a matter of belief than faith."

I am in complete agreement with that statement and this is why I feel another danger in the socialization model. It can easily be content with the internalization of beliefs. A very active member of the Church can have deep convictions about the dogmas, rituals, and laws of the Church like the Marxist can have about Marxist dogmas, rituals, and laws if the internalization of the symbol system has worked in both cases. But a conviction, resulting from successful internalization of exterior or "objectified" realities, is not the same thing as faith. They have to do with two different levels of human experience.

Ideological internalization is part of religion and I have nothing against it, but it is not faith. The problem is that while being of different nature they are intimately and, for our power of discernment at least, probably inextricably linked. Therefore my point is that, formed by the socialization model, we may easily lose sight of the fact that our concern as educators is not only with internalization of beliefs but also, or mainly, with growth in faith. Or we may easily think that while encouraging the first we are necessarily working for the second. This brings me to my last point.

- *By the nature of its ultimate criteria the socialization model is tempted to overlook the radically personal and spiritual dimension of religious experience and faith.*

This last critique deals with the same problem as the second one but it tries to clarify it a little more and look at it from a slightly different angle.

Berard writes: "The ultimate success of the socialization process must be judged . . . by answering how well adults are assimilated into the faith community and how closely they identify with it." At the end of his paper he is more precise: ". . . how well they understand and carry on the mission of Christ in the world." In the course of the paper though, dealing with personal faith, he did mention that "the goal of catechesis is maturity of faith." He also mentioned growth in personal faith as one of the threefold goals of religious education.

In brief we know that for Berard and in his socialization model, growth in faith, maturity of faith, are *part of* the "ultimate success" that is described in terms of assimilation into and identification with the Church.

My problem then with the way things are presented here is first that one can seem to have reached the ultimate criteria of assimilation and identification even if the growth in personal faith has not been achieved. And second, authentic growth in faith can occur without necessarily leading to assimilation into and identification with the Church, at least in the sense it is presented in the model.

The second part of the statement is pretty obvious. We all know adults who are deeply spiritual and committed Christians really living the Gospel in their personal and sometimes communal life but who for one reason or another do not feel they are or want to be assimilated into or identified with any specific church. The *religious* aspects of their life are—according to certain criteria—incomplete but they are living a *real faith* life.

As for the first part of my statement it is more complex and requires more explication. As it is, for me, very fundamental, I will now attempt to describe what I mean in some detail.

Among the excellent things he writes about personal faith, Berard brings in a quotation from Rahner: Education in faith means "to assist understanding of *what has already been experienced in the depths of human reality as grace* (i.e., as in absolutely direct relation to God)" (italics mine).

I could not agree more with Rahner and my point is precisely that if that initial, preconceptual—I would tend to say "poetic"—religious experience has not been made then our religious education is building a house without foundations. What I am also saying is that the socialization model can easily be misleading here. I see in it a potential danger inasmuch as it could very easily lead a child or an adult through the various assimilation-identification phases even if the foundation is missing. And this is the case because the model works, as Berard well described it, according to the dialectical pattern of externalization, objectification and internalization, which functions at a different level of experience from the one we refer to when we are talking about faith.

In other words the socialization model can very well function purely on a religious level that would not include real faith: personal encounter and relationship with God. In such a case there would be religious behaviors—knowledge, beliefs, rituals, norms, activities, and so forth—without any faith experience. The religious belonging would be only (instead of also) an ideological belonging, which I feel it should not be. This brings to light a fundamental ambiguity in the model. On the one hand it has "more to do with beliefs than faith," as Berard notes, and on the other it pretends to include "growth in faith" as one of its goals.

These reflections, I believe, then lead us to question the value of the criteria of success ascribed to the educational enterprise as assimilation into and identification with the Church.

Conclusion

As I have made clear, I think Berard's presentation of the socialization model is and will be a significant contribution to the progress of religious education in the years to come. Of course, as Berard says himself, presenting a model is only a first step and a great deal of work remains to be done to improve it, enrich it, and make it operative. It is to help eventually with this second step in the work that I would like to make the following suggestions or at least to express my wishes and hopes!

I hope Berard will consider explicitly "building into" his model the critical dimension of shared praxis because I sincerely believe that if that dimension is missing the socialization model can be dangerous for the quality and authenticity of religious education and also of life in the Church, whereas if it is included I think it can have a very deep and far-reaching liberating and transforming influence not only in education but for the renewal of the Church.

If Berard would consider making that move it would hopefully bring him to modify the decidedly assimilative vocabulary he used throughout his presentation, vocabulary that in itself induces the corresponding educational attitudes. I think that in this area the dialogue between Tom and Berard could be most fruitful.

I also hope that another model could be worked out some day that would better bring to light the deeply personal and spiritual character of faith inasmuch as it is a lived relationship with the Divine Persons. The two models would complement each other. Even before we have such a model I would find it very important that the aspects mentioned above would be emphasized and that the risks I have described would be brought to the attention of those who would be working in the framework of the socialization model.

Finally I think that the socialization model could also be improved if it took into consideration what Gabe Moran is saying about teaching religion "from a distance." On this I will comment in the last part of this essay.

Gabriel Moran: Where Now, What Next

Introduction

As I mentioned at the beginning of this essay, each panelist understood the topic of the symposium in a very different way. Gabe Moran in his paper, as in most of his writings, touched upon many very fundamental and complex questions; in doing so he criticized the use we make of current language, which was a surprise for no one! As is often the case with the writings of great people, you are never quite sure you have really understood them. It is always risky then to take the position of critical reactor. However, after listening to Gabe during the two days' conversation I think I understood his paper better and felt encouraged in the attempt to present my reaction to two main points he brought up.

I think for Gabe what is foundational for the future of religious education is not theory or method or operational model but structure. I also believe that for him this structural problem is linked to a language problem—I should rather say many language problems!

During the symposium Gabe was indeed attacked on the language problem, but the structural question was hardly discussed, although it had for me very important implications. I intend here to discuss the structural question he raised in presenting the two "settings" he advocates for religious education. Then I would like to come back to the very controversial language problem about revelation.

1. Discussion of Gabe Moran's Proposed Structure for Religious Education

Jim Lee and Gabe Moran were the only ones to explicitly mention structural problems in their papers. For Jim, religious education could be structured along three lines: administration, counseling, and instruction. Gabe disagrees with the notion of education as expressed in these divisions. The structure he proposes for religious education is built around two settings, each including several orientations.

"The two settings," he writes, "I call 'school' and 'laboratory' (a word I'm not entirely happy with, but one connoting work, joint activity, and experiments)."

My purpose here is not to discuss the overall institutional problems involved in reorganizing the whole national scene of religious education around either Jim's or Gabe's propositions. This is a mammoth problem not at stake here. However, I would like to mention that to me neither of these structural systems would be adequate. What I would like to do is to comment on the two settings Gabe proposes for our attention. I will deal first with the "laboratory" setting, then with the "school" setting.

● *Discussion of the "laboratory" setting:*

Although I don't like the word "laboratory," which strangely enough does have manipulative connotations, I understand what Gabe means and agree that education can indeed go on in the three main orientations he describes under laboratory: the family/community, the work site, the retreat.

Let me point out here a problem we always have in reading Gabe: We are never sure of what age bracket he is referring to. Most often he speaks of education in reference to adolescents or adults and those of us who have children in mind misunderstand him!

Here we have the same problem. Obviously when he talks about "the study of religion from within (often called theology by the Church)," he is not referring to children but a few lines before or after he does and this is confusing. This is why I am going to bring in age precisions when I think they are necessary so that we can understand what and who we are talking about.

● *The family/community setting:*

Gabe recognizes the importance of that setting but asks us not to overburden the family. I agree with him and have many times expressed my disagreement with the mushrooming of pre-school home programs for children of three to five years of age. I believe that the formative influence at this stage should be only the intrinsic quality of family life. Gabe wrote one day: "It is enough to establish small children in a universe of Christian charity."[7] I would complete this statement with other aspects but fundamentally I agree with it for children up to six.

However I do feel that it is not overburdening families to ask them to take their full responsibility during the decisive years of early Christian initiative. Going around the country in the past decade, I have seen more and more evidence that when families are helped in the right way to take over this responsibility it benefits not only the children but, at least as much, the parents themselves.

Furthermore, bringing families together to take an active part in the sacramental initiation of their children often contributes to the development of those "communal surroundings" Gabe is asking the Church to provide.

I also support Gabe's preoccupation that everything not be centered on families. We indeed have to encourage the emergence of communal surroundings that include all categories of persons. But when Gabe writes, "Church officials should provide communal surroundings for families and for the majority of people who do not live in father-mother-children units," I would like to stress that community cannot be created by any authoritative decision. It begins to exist when people who want it effectively enter the process of building it.

● *The work-site setting:*

Unfortunately Gabe never described this setting. He mentioned it twice—once in his opening statement, then, in passing, he suggested that for him work in this context was social action (p. 18). I think it is a pity he did not develop this because it is perhaps the most original part of his suggestions. So, I hope Gabe won't mind if I take this opportunity to develop this idea in my own way.

I do think for the young and adults the work site can be an extremely important setting for education. However, for me, this work site would be not only social action but any kind of project people come together to carry out for the service of the community, be it social, political, educational, recreational, or whatever.

Any kind of common action is an ideal site for education—I should say, can become an ideal site, because it is far from being automatic.

Two conditions, I think, make it possible. First, that the people not be mere executants, carrying out someone else's project, be it the pastor's as docile instruments or whatever. Second, the participants themselves must want their endeavor to be, at one and the same time, a service to the community and an educational opportunity for them. If this is the case, their group would be a "reflection-action-oriented group" or a responsibility-oriented group. They would get involved in some project of their own making, related to their real lives, to their social environment, to their concrete responsibilities. That working group should develop what Paulo Freire calls a critical consciousness and Tom Groome's shared-praxis method could provide a basic orientation for its functioning with the difference that the direct confrontation with reality—in the project they are actually carrying on together—would give the whole enterprise a much greater impact and also present extra requirements (an exploration phase of the concrete milieu for instance). You learn best by doing. And it would be in the very process of action/reflection that they would discover the actuality of God's call here and now and the power of his Spirit.

It is my deep conviction that the real effective religious adult education group is one that, through the development of a critical consciousness, becomes capable all at once of deepening its own religious experience, and of initiating and carrying out effective action. It is through that very experience that people will rediscover the real meaning of their belonging to the Church—not as a privilege but as a responsibility—and will effectively build the Church, the type of Church that will make sense for the young generation. I don't think we have as yet realized in this country the transforming power of such groups within the Church. We have reflection or prayer groups on the one hand, we have preorganized action groups on the other. But the power of the "free mixture" is tremendous.

One can wonder why we have so few of these groups comparative to other types of groups. One reason is perhaps that we feel vaguely threatened by the very power that would rest in the hands of such groups. The assimilation aspect of the socialization model here would certainly be overpowered by the transforming one! The other reason is that we have very few, if any, educators who are trained and prepared to encourage the development of such groups and act as facilitators for them.[8] This again is where I feel the diffusion of Tom Groome's shared-praxis method among educators could be extremely beneficial.

To conclude this long development I would like to reiterate then my agreement with Gabe on the importance of the work-site setting for effective learning in religious education.

● *The retreat setting:*

Concerning retreats Gabe writes: "The contemplative element, which is appropriate to the retreat and complementary to liturgy, cannot be directly taught; nonetheless it is at the center of all education." I fully support this statement and the need for places in our cities where people can not only get into "programmed retreats" but also and even mainly, as Gabe says, "step back . . . and be quiet" within themselves. I will not develop this here because I will come back to it in my conclusion. But I would like to state the fact that Gabe is the only panelist, it seems to me, who explicitly stressed the importance of that contemplative dimension in education.

He is also the only one—and the conjunction of both these facts is significant—who seemed to be really in touch with the "outer world," meaning the nonecclesiastical world, helping us to look "beyond our village." This brings me to the second part of this analysis dealing with Gabe's first setting for religious education: the school.

● *The school setting:*[9]

Before discussing this topic I would like to express my partial agreement with Gabe on another but related issue. I do think that on a graduate level in religious education the "academic, scholarly, and rational" aspect has not been sufficiently emphasized. As much as I feel that we have been right to move away from that aspect in early religious education, so do I believe that in late undergraduate and graduate programs that aspect has been underestimated. There is an urgent need for greater academic quality on the graduate level and for much more serious initiation to scientific methodology in the areas of theology, biblical studies, and also the related social sciences. This is not in my opinion the only requirement of graduate religious education "from within." It should also include, I believe, a communal experience and practical supervised experiments, but the quality of the academic aspect is a fundamental one indeed.

Concerning what Gabe calls "religious education from a distance," I fully agree with him that "there are millions of people today who are dissaffiliated with confessional religious language, but who are very interested in religious experience and the diversity of religious traditions. They want to hear about religion "from a different point of view than from within a church and with church language." Here is how Gabe describes that teaching from a distance: ". . . a way of speaking about religion which includes a coalition of many different sciences and arts than that which has gone under the name of catholic or protestant theologies would be part of the whole picture."

In the past ten years in Canada and namely in Quebec we have been facing an increasing demand for that kind of teaching. The very fact that we are struggling to find the proper names for this new "field" (if it is a field!) is indicative of the novelty of the perspective. At the undergraduate level such programs are called "Religious Culture." At the graduate level we talk about "Religious Sciences" or "Study of Religions" or even "Religiology," all these terms trying to describe different approaches to what we could call "the religious phenomenon." This teaching from a distance could include phenomenology, sociology, psychology of religion and history of religions through art, oral and written traditions, and so forth.

My own limited experience in teaching a very elementary course in Psychology of Religious Experience has been a fascinating one. I had students from two different horizons. Some were regular students from the theology department working for their B.A. Others were students from other departments who took the course as an option just for interest in religion. Most of those were what we call "outsiders" searching for a better understanding of religious experience. I was personally very enriched by my contacts and discussions with these students and I think that for both categories of students it was very significant to be able to reflect on their experiences from the point of view of a nonpartisan critical science. The Christian students who felt a little threatened at first experienced a real liberation. They had to face the challenge of questions coming from the "outsiders." These questions, they discovered, were often extremely relevant and coincided with questions they had never dared ask themselves! The so-called "outsiders" were amazed at discovering both the differences and similarities of their own experiences with those of the Christian students. And all were very interested in understanding better the psychological foundations of religious experience that demythologizes certain things but leaves open the space for questioning about God. For the Christian students I think it was a "purifying" experience and for all a maturing one.

This is just an example to explain why I fully support Gabe's preoccupation with "teaching from a distance." However, I believe that programs studying religion from a distance should not be called religious education. This would be confusing, considering our most common recent usage of the word meaning "education from within a tradition."

As the example I gave demonstrates, we have two kinds of people interested in such courses, those who are studying to be religious educators in their church and those who are interested in studying religions and related phenomena but who do not wish to be religiously educated. The two purposes are very different and should be respected for what they are. Practically the best structure to ensure this respect would probably be to set up a separate independent program of religious studies or whatever one wants to call it. Some students would be only in that program. Others, coming from the religious education department, would take some courses in the other program. This structure wherever it would be possible would allow us to serve the needs of people "beyond our village."

2. *The Language Problem Concerning Gabe's Idea of Revelation*

Right away some readers will react to this subtitle by saying that it is not a language problem, but a much deeper one; I agree it is not only a language problem but it is *also* one.

Tom Groome accused Gabe of having a post-Christian idea of revelation. Others told Tom his idea was neoorthodox! I do not intend to discuss the overall theological question involved here nor to identify with either of these labelings. But I would like to express my support for Gabe's effort to try to find a language that can cut across our barriers and be meaningful to those who are in "another community of discourse." When Berard used this expression to designate the people Gabe was trying to talk to, he seemed to imply that doing this was fine with him, but that it had not much to do with Berard's own preoccupation with religious education; this is what I would like to challenge.

I think it does have a tremendous importance if we are to stop talking only to ourselves! After all the "Good News" is for all. I am convinced that the way Gabe is trying to talk about revelation is much more meaningful for those millions of people we were talking about formerly who are so estranged from our Church linguistic universe.

If I understand him correctly, Gabe is saying that he thinks of revelation as "that in which all humans participate, that which points to what is universal in human experience." He also states that he "uses the word revelation as a description of the relational structure of reality," that "it is because reality is relational that it is revelatory." Then he talks about specific "embodiments" of that revelation and says: "Not only do I accept but I demand a biblical, or Christian or Roman Catholic expression or embodiment of that revelation," stressing the "uniqueness of that revelation in Christ." This language, of course, is a little disturbing to those who feel secure in the neatly packaged description of general and special revelation. It is perhaps a more poetic than technical language, but this is probably why it could be more meaningful for people who are unfamiliar with ecclesiastical language.[10]

Just to illustrate this I would like to bring together for mutual enlightenment Gabe's description of revelation and its different "embodiments" with the quotation from Rahner that was used by Berard in his paragraphs on faith.

According to Rahner, what we do in religious education is to "assist understanding of what has already been experienced in the depth of human reality as grace (i.e., as in absolutely direct relation to God)." Is not that language strikingly similar to that of Moran describing the depth of reality as both and inseparably relational and revelatory? Could we then attempt to describe things in the following way: When, through my own personal experience, I come in touch with the depth of reality, it reveals itself as relational, as open to the possibility of an unnamed Presence. Then, to interpret this experience and bring it to maturity, I will look to the various traditions that have over the centuries embodied innumerable such experiences. Among them are the Christian traditions and churches. For us, the uniqueness of our Christian Tradition is that it embodies the radically unique experience of that man Jesus in whom the word was made flesh and to whom the first Christian communities bore witness:

> That which was from the beginning, which we have heard, which we have seen with our eyes, which we have looked upon and touched with our hands, concerning the word of life—the life was made manifest, and we saw it, and testify to it, and proclaim to you the eternal life which was with the Father and was made manifest to us—that which we have seen and heard we proclaim also to you, so that you may have fellowship with us; and our fellowship is with the Father and with his Son Jesus Christ. And we are writing this that our joy may be complete.
> This is the message we have heard from him and proclaim to you, that God is light and in him is no darkness at all (1 Jn. 1:1-5).

The foundational event through which the Christian churches interpret their experience of reality is the very experience of Jesus who through his life, death, and resurrection manifested that indeed the very structure of reality is relational, rooted as it is in the mystery of God as Father, Son, and Spirit.

I don't know what Gabe will think of these personal "variations" on the way he treats the revelation theme. My point is only that I feel Gabe is right when he is trying to find a language—and language shapes the concepts of course—that will cut across the barriers separating the "Church people" from those who are searching on their own for a faith that will give meaning to their deepest experiences.

Conclusion

Gabe Moran is disturbing because he never ceases to upset our "ready-made ideas" that are, as the French philosopher Edgar Morin writes, "as undegradable as plastic waste." He also critiques our language to a point that sometimes irritates us. It is as if he were disarming us for any verbal confrontation with him! All this is true, but this is exactly why Gabe has been and is so important to those of us who are working in religious education. He forces us to think!

At this symposium Gabe's main contribution touched two very important points. He explicitly brought to our attention the contemplative dimension of religious education. And he constantly tried to remind us that we have to look "beyond our village," and create a language that will build bridges instead of building barriers. To do this we have to listen to those we think are "outside." But who really knows after all who is "outside" and who is "inside"?

General Conclusion: The Challenge Ahead of Us

Coming to the end of the "impossible task" that was assigned to me, I would like to express my gratitude to my fellow panelists. In trying to critically analyze their papers and taped conversations I have been not only informed but considerably enriched. And if I have, as probable, misunderstood or misinterpreted some of their ideas, I will be happy to pursue with them that open and friendly dialogue.

To conclude this essay I will not present a synthesis of my own ideas. Many of them I had a chance to express along the way and it would be fastidious. I will rather, as I said in the beginning, express my fears and my hopes and attempt to point out some important aspects of the challenge that lies ahead of us.

Concerning the vocabulary of religious education, each panelist has a different view on the matter and I will by no means try to settle the dispute. However I would like to state a fact: Whatever our preferences, the word "catechetics" is likely to stay with us for a while simply because it is going to be "officialized," if I might say, in the *National Catechetical Directory*. So, personally I do not think it is worthwhile or wise to fight against it. However, since for me and others catechetics is only one part of religious education, I would like to see the latter term stay alive. But I do think we should give it more precision by qualifying it according to the context in which we are using it.

Talking about the *National Catechetical Directory* let me also express my fears and my hopes. The uniquely democratic way in which the consultations were made is in itself an achievement. Nevertheless when the finished product comes out very soon my fear is that, for many people, it will be the end of questioning and searching. It is so much easier and more reassuring to be told what to do! I do hope it will not be promoted or interpreted in a too directive and normative perspective. I also hope that, while making full use of the very valuable help it will bring us, we will all remain constructively critical of its content and outcomes. I hope we will not betray its spirit and that we will receive it as a stimulation for renewed research and creativity.

Research and creativity, yes; indeed this is, in my opinion, the challenge ahead of us! I think the symposium, to which some people came with the dream of receiving a neatly packaged synthesis of theology, psychology, and pedagogy, has sharply brought out the complexity of the problems and the areas of knowledge involved in religious education. This in itself made the endeavor worthwhile.

The symposium was supposed to deal with foundational questions in religious education. Some were touched upon —none in depth—and some of the most important ones were not even mentioned. This is why I would like to simply enumerate some of them so that we can envisage the work ahead of us.

It might be helpful to classify these problems in two groups dealing with two different aspects or areas of concern. All classification is arbitrary of course but this one fits my purpose.

- *Foundational problems related to the intellectual aspects of religious education*

These problems concern basically the relation between catechetics and different sciences.

— What is actually and what should be the relation between catechetics and the modern scriptural sciences? To what extent and how, at different age levels, should catechetics take

into account the work of these sciences?
— The same question should be asked regarding theology. Saying that catechetics has to do with doctrine and not theology is a fallacy as I said before. Any doctrinal presentation is inspired by and framed into a theology, even if implicitly.
— The same question again pertains to the relation between catechetics and some critical social sciences, namely sociology, depth psychology, and linguistics. Superficial use of those sciences is frequent, but real, honest acceptance of the radical questions they confront us with has hardly begun.

● *Foundational problems related to the pastoral aspects of religious education*

Many of the questions discussed at the symposium were "how" questions. The real foundational questions though are most often "why" or "what" questions. Moreover, as Gabe Moran pointed out, religious education problems are often church problems. Indeed this is why they are pastoral problems. Many could be mentioned here but I will only bring out those that seem to me more crucial in our present situation.

— Why should we or should we not continue to baptize infants and then attempt to socialize them into the Church till their first communion only to see them vanish right after?
— Why are we so reluctant to consider the relevance of a much more progressive and slow process of socialization that would spread the sacramentalization of children over a longer period of time, allowing for an eventual common religious evolution of a family?
— In more general terms we could ask: What should be the relation between evangelization and catechetics? Should the second always necessarily follow the first? Do we really understand the fact underlined by Vatican II that there are different degrees of belonging to the Church?
— What is our educational responsibility toward those "beyond our village," whom we should not try to "socialize into the Church" but still should serve?

In my opinion these are some of the foundational questions we should face in religious education today. All other questions dealing with structures, theories, models, and methods are also important but they should not divert our attention from those that are even more serious because they are more foundational.

As it is obvious to anyone reading these last paragraphs, we are indeed brought back to another both general and foundational question, which is that of our vision of the Church. What we will or will not do in religious education in the years to come depends finally and fundamentally on our image of the Church. This is why I feel it is so important that all those trying to address basic or foundational questions in religious education be asked to spell out as a background their vision of the Church. An open dialogue around this topic would be basic to further discussion on religious education and would considerably enlighten and clarify the more practical problems.

Finally, after all that talk about structures, theories, models, and problems, may none of us ever forget that what is really at stake here is, as an ancient patristic tradition beautifully said, that "God may be born into man's heart." When that happens it is always a unique but never isolated revelatory experience. Once it has happened everything becomes possible and unpredictable. This is why I agree that "revelation is the last word before silence" (G. Moran).

Notes

1. This statement comes from the belief paper called "Opening Remarks" that Jim distributed at the symposium.

2. God should not be thought of as "someone out there." His transcendence is not a transcendence of exteriority but of interiority.

3. Concerning this statement, Tom refers to two authors: in this paper, to Jose Ortega y Gasset, *What is Philosophy*, and in his *Lumen Vitae* article to Paul Ricoeur, *Freud and Philosophy*. But I think this reference is not totally relevant here precisely because the two authors he mentions were talking about reflection in a philosophical and not a praxeological context.

4. A. Dumoulin and J. M. Jaspard, *Les mediations religieuses dans l'univers de l'enfant* (Bruxelles: Editions *Lumen Vitae*, 1972).

5. C. Ellis Nelson, *Where Faith Begins* (Richmond, Va.: John Knox Press, 1967), p. 202.

6. Editor's note: See James Fowler, "Faith Development Theory

and the Aims of Religious Socialization," in *Emerging Issues in Religious Education*, Gloria Durka and Joanmarie Smith, eds. (New York: Paulist Press, 1976).

7. G. Moran, *Catechesis of Revelation* (New York: Herder and Herder, 1966), p. 118.

8. If I may, I would like to introduce here two personal comments. The first is that at the Department of Pastoral Studies in Montreal we have developed a praxeological model for the training of those students who want to get into pastoral work. The second is that six years ago my husband and I put out with Paulist Press an Adult Education Program for Parents that proposed in effect a praxis approach. This is the only book we published that was not well received and we thought it could be the most important and effective one! It was certainly too demanding for a first try. But I think one of the reasons for its failure was the lack of preparation to understand the method among religious educators. The few places where it was fruitful were those where facilitators were really prepared and grasped the effectiveness of the method. (cf. *To Be A Parent* [New York: Paulist Press]).

9. Let us make an important distinction here. We are not talking about children but only about young people in their late teens and adults.

10. Moran does not dismiss this more ecclesiastical language as "wrong"; he only says it is not helpful.